India's New Development Agenda

Dr. N.A. Mujumdar is former Principal Adviser, Reserve Bank of India. At present, he is the Editor of the Indian Journal of Agricultural Economics and also Honorary Professor at the Society for Development Studies.

Dr. Mujumdar began his career as Lecturer in what was then known as the School of Economics, University of Bombay. He was Nuffield Fellow of Oxford University, Oxford, in 1959, and after his return to India, joined the Reserve Bank of India.

The author has also worked, under the auspices of the International Monetary Fund, as Adviser to the Central Banks of five countries: Zambia, Mauritius, Tanzania, Belize and Cambodia. He was Consultant to FAO, ESCAP and the World Bank. He was member of various Working Groups appointed by the Reserve Bank of India and the Planning Commission.

He has published various books and a number of research papers in various technical journals. Among his recent books are: *Economic Reforms Sans Development* (2004), *Indian Agriculture in the New Millennium* (a set of 2 volumes co-edited with Uma Kapila, 2006) and *Inclusive Growth: Development Perspectives in Indian Economy* (2007) published by Academic Foundation, New Delhi.

India's New Development Agenda

Building a Value-based Society

N.A. MUJUMDAR

ACADEMIC FOUNDATION
NEW DELHI

www.academicfoundation.com

First published in 2011
by

ACADEMIC FOUNDATION
4772-73 / 23 Bharat Ram Road, (23 Ansari Road),
Darya Ganj, New Delhi - 110 002 (India).
Phones : 23245001 / 02 / 03 / 04.
Fax : +91-11-23245005.
E-mail : books@academicfoundation.com
www. academicfoundation.com

Cataloging in Publication Data--DK
Courtesy: D.K. Agencies (P) Ltd. docinfo@dkagencies.com

Mujumdar, N.A.
India's new development agenda : building a value-based society / N.A. Mujumdar.
p. cm.
Includes index.
ISBN 13: 9788171888818
ISBN 10: 817188881X

1. Economic development--India. 2. Monetary policy--India. 3. Financial crisis--India. 4. India--Economic policy--1991- I. Title.

DDC 338.954 22

Typeset by Italics India, New Delhi.
Printed and bound in India.

To my grand-daughter Medha

Contents

Part III
Monetary and Credit Policies

Part IV
Global Financial Crisis and India

Part V
The Agricultural Sector

Introduction

The global financial and economic crisis of 2008 was ferocious and it has changed dramatically the institutional and policymaking landscape. But some of our own 'reformers' and 'lobbyists' seem to refuse to learn from this global experience. For Daniel Kahneman, who was awarded the Nobel Prize in Economics in 2002, the most moving episode in the current global economic crisis took place when a humbled Alan Greenspan, the former Chairman of the US Federal Reserve, confessed before a Congressional Committee that he had put too much faith in the self-correcting power of free markets. 'He basically said that the framework within which we had been operating was false, and coming from Greenspan, that was impressive'. The basic belief in the magical power of the market to discipline itself and yield good outcomes has been shattered. (IMF, 2009).

This is a defining moment in the history of global economic system. The collapse in 2008 of the capitalist model of the American economy was as traumatic as the collapse of the communist model of Russia in 1991. We have thus arrived at a moment in world economic history, when the disillusionment with the centrally planned economies is matched by the loss of faith in the capitalist system led by unbridled market forces. We in India have already discarded the centrally planned economic model and adopted the capitalist model since 1991 and if we now disown the capitalist model, where do we go from here?

What lessons do we derive from the 2008 global crisis? We may not have our own Reagonomics or Thatcherism to bury: but some of our contemporary policymakers and lobbyists are soaked in the market theology of IMF/World Bank. It would not be easy to disengage them from the trappings of market theology and induce them to refrain from mimicking the Western models. Look at the current lobbying for the so-called 'reforms' which essentially include, disinvestments; privatisation of public sector banks (PSBs); a bigger role for foreign direct investment (FDI) in retail, insurance, aviation and banking; dilution of government equity in profitably state-run entities: merger of associate banks of State Bank of India with the parent bank so that this bank could become internationally competitive, based on the principle 'too big to fail'; making Mumbai an international financial centre where multinationals could freely enter, and so on. Are the ghosts of market theologians of IMF/World Bank still haunting some of our reformers and articulate lobbyists? One would have thought that in the post-collapse phase of the American capitalist model, one should be convinced that there is no intellectual support for privatisation *per se*. Economic efficiency is ownership-neutral. In a broader context, do we need to rewrite the script of development economics?

Based on the more recent development experience of the Indian economy during the period 1991 to 2008, the 30 chapters in this book, seek to provide an answer to this broader question. The answer is that we must grow up from the conventional growth economics trapped in market theology to resonate to the larger concerns of holistic development.

These larger concerns include promotion of broad-based, decentralised growth which alone could facilitate access by the poor to employment, food, nutrition and health, and quality education; and to putting in place appropriate safety nets to reduce the vulnerability of the poor; and above all, to build a value-based society. Figuratively speaking, this entails journey from Milton Friedman to Mahatma Gandhi.

It is an irony of economic history that India which was a pioneer in emphasising 'growth with equity' in its approach to development, much before mainstream development economists caught up with it, should have relapsed into a phase of mindless pursuit of market theology preached by IMF/World Bank. This period of economic reforms from 1991 to 2004 was the most retrogressive phase, a phase which I have called the Milton Friedman phase. Although India graduated to a high-growth league during this phase, it had to pay a heavy price. While wealth accumulated, men decayed. The number of underfed and undernourished people in India rose from 206 million to 230 million during the period. According to the National Family Health Survey of 2005-06 (NFHS-3), almost half of the children under the age of five are stunted, or too short for their age and 43 per cent are underweight. The survey finds that the primary cause is inadequate intake of food, leading to, in some cases, chronic and acute undernutrition.

The growth culture itself became toxic during this period. A huge quantity of food grains was exported, at a time when the number of underfed persons increased. Policymakers of the time condemned subsidies for domestic consumption of food grains: but they had no qualms about subsidising exports of food grains. The interest rate regime which emerged as a result of financial sector reforms pampered the corporate elite and discriminated against small borrowers generally. This inequity in interest rates was compounded by fiscal inequity designed to pamper the dividend-earning elite. In the book I wrote earlier I had demonstrated that economic reforms introduced since 1991 had diluted the development content (Mujumdar, 2004). The analysis in the present book shows clearly that the reformers soaked in market theology went further in this direction and reforms degenerated into the anti-development instruments. While there is enough literature on the harm inflicted on the economy by the centrally planned economic phase—the so-called licence permit raj—little attention has been paid to the negative impact of the pursuit of unbridled market philosophy during the 1991-2004 phase. Economic historians need to pay greater attention to the unsavoury aspect. It is interesting to add here that the macroeconomic highway to growth—better known as the 'Washington Consensus'—stands discredited today.

The launching of the Bharat Nirman programme in 2005 marked a radical departure from the Milton Friedman phase. It appears that Indian policymakers began to rediscover Mahatma Gandhi. There was the mid-day meal programme for school children, provision of nutritional supplements to children upto the age of six years, and so on. The National Rural Employment Guarantee Act (NREGA), 2005 was the best that could have happened to the rural poor. The culmination of this journey towards holistic development is the proposed National Food Security Act. I have therefore called this phase the Mahatma Gandhi phase.

As the recent growth report emphasises, there is no generic formula for growth. 'Each country has specific characteristics and historical experiences that must be reflected in its growth strategy' (World Bank, 2008). We must overcome our obsession with replicating 'international best practices' and evolve our own model which resonates to India-specific needs. In fact this has already happened in the case of our financial system.

India has a well-diversified financial system dominated by the public sector institutions: commercial banks, cooperative banks, non-banking financial institutions (NBFIs) and the insurance sector. Commercial banks dominated by PSBs together with cooperative banks account for nearly 70 per cent of the total assets of the Indian financial system.

Over the years, there has taken place significant financial deepening: this is reflected in credit-GDP and liquid liabilities (M3)-GDP ratios. What is more, this financial deepening has resulted in a dramatic rise in savings rate. The rate of domestic savings has shot up from 23.5 per cent of GDP in 2001-02 to 37.7 per cent in 2007-08. This in turn facilitated the step-up in investment rate from 22.8 per cent to 39.1 per cent during the period. India's growth story is thus primarily the story of domestic savings and this in turn is to a large extent the story of PSB's contribution to bolstering domestic savings.

The global financial crisis has had understandably a catastrophic impact on bank credit in the US and in Europe. Not so in India. There was high growth in credit deployment by the banking sector; credit expanded at an average annual rate of around 30 per cent during the three years before the global crisis. In a way, we have now gone beyond 'international best practices' and evolved our own model which resonates to the needs of the real sector. Amidst all the chorus for privatisation, it is to the credit of the Reserve Bank of India (RBI) that they have openly commended upon the Indian banking model: 'Indian Banking is a success story in the midst of the financially triggered global crisis of 2008 thanks to the regulatory environment in place and the structural banking drivers' (RBI, 2009). RBI states with pride that Indian banking has many practices which are worth emulating by other countries.

The Indian financial system dominated by the public sector has thus made us proud. At a time when banks in the US and Europe went through 'a near-death experience', to borrow a phrase from Ben Bernanke, the current Chairman of Federal Reserve, US, 'our banks held their heads high'.

Again, take the Satyam case. It is a unique story of how a company with a $1.8 billion hole in its balance sheet—hole made by private greed in its ugliest form—was turned around in 100 days through Government intervention. The technocrats chosen by the governments to handle this transformation have emerged as the new Schumpeterian heroes (Economic Times, 2009).

Not merely lack of regulatory mechanism, as some apologists of today's capitalism seem to be arguing, but unbridled greed seems to be at the root of the fall of the capitalist model—predatory capitalist model—be it Enron of yesteryears or American banks during the 2008 crisis. Perhaps the very nature of the governance culture of private corporate sector is such that it breeds unbridled greed. This volume thus takes us well beyond growth models. Evolving a value-based compassionate society for which Mahatma Gandhi struggled involves betterment of the individual whose life must be guided by the three 'Da's'—*damyata*, *datta* and *dayadhvam*: practice self-control, charity, and compassion. Here we move from development models to the realm of economic philosophy of development.

Does this new approach to what I have called 'holistic development' warrant the evolution of a new version of development economics? How do we need to modify, in the light of the new objective, our development agenda, both in the real and financial sector reforms? Incidentally, it is quite clear how incongruous the current demands of some 'reformers' for privatisation look, when judged by the new objective. Finally, how do we superimpose a value-based societal framework on the modified development agenda? The chapters in the book seek to provide answers to these questions. I would be happy if this book could provoke further thinking in this direction.

Finally, a personal note about my association with the Academic Foundation. This association dates back to 2002 when they published my book *Financial Sector Reforms and India's Economic Development* (2002). All along these years Dr. (Mrs.) Uma Kapila has taken a personal interest in the publication of my books and articles. I am most grateful to her and to her colleagues in the organisation.

— N.A. Mujumdar

Part I
Approaches to Development

1 Mainstream Development Economics and the Eleventh Plan

The idioms and metaphors of development economics seem to be changing from time to time. The Approach Paper to the Eleventh Five-Year Plan (2007-08 to 2011-12) aims at putting the economy in a sustainable growth trajectory with a growth rate of approximately 10 per cent in the terminal year, which would yield an average growth rate of about 9 per cent in the Plan period. But the Plan document admits: 'yet, it is also true that economic growth has failed to be sufficiently inclusive particularly after the mid-1990s' (Planning Commission, 2006: 1). Rapid growth is an essential part of strategy for growth and development. 'This must be combined with policies that will ensure that per capita income is broad based, benefiting all sections of population, especially these who have thus far remained deprived'. (Ibid.: 2).

This new-found concern for growth with equity shows that development economics has come a long way from its earlier position. Indian researchers would recall that in the 1950s when the Indian Planning Commission sought to build equity into the development plan, the mainstream development economists scoffed at the idea. Their dictum was: enlarge the size of the national income cake; distribution will take care of itself. These were the hey-days of the percolation or trickle-down theory of growth. In contrast, more recently, there is a bumper harvest of Reports of international institutions and development discourse by eminent economists emphasising complementarity between equity and development. The UN Report on 'Investing in Development: A Practical Plan to Achieve the Millennium Development Goals' (2005). The *Human Development Report 2006*, on 'Beyond Scarcity: Power, Poverty and Global Water Crisis', and the recent book by Jeffrey D. Sachs, whom the New York Magazine described 'as probably the most important economist in the

World', *The End of Poverty: Economic Possibilities for Our Time* (2005), are instances in point. As a culmination of these discourses on development is the *World Development Report 2006*, entitled 'Equity and Development'. The Report puts it categorically: 'Because our ultimate goal is the reduction of poverty through the equitable pursuit of prosperity, the policy suggestions in these chapters are consistent with good poverty reduction policies...' (World Bank, 2005: 23). Equity, as many scholars have recognised, is intrinsically important as a development goal in its own right. But as the World Bank President Paul D. Wolfowitz argues, 'this Report goes further by presenting evidence that a sharing of economic and political opportunities is also instrumental for economic growth and development' (Foreword: vii). In other words, equity reinforces the growth process itself. To an extent, this shift in emphasis was influenced by the 'shared growth' experience of Asian Tigers. The Approach Paper of the Eleventh Plan perhaps responds to this more recent change of emphasis on equity in the development discourse. One may also add that it also reflects a sort of penance of Indian policymakers of the 1990s who, as enthusiastic disciples of the market theology of IMF/World committed many mistakes. Neglect of agriculture, deceleration in public investment in agriculture, disdain for subsidies, whether food subsidy or credit subsidy, focussing on jobless growth, disregard of the elementary principles of food security—these are among the major pit-falls of policies pursued in the 1990s. I have documented them elsewhere (Mujumdar, 2004).

The most conspicuous example of mindless pursuit of market theology leading to policy blunders is in the area of food security. Following IMF/World Bank prescriptions, Indian policymakers cut down food subsidies in the 1990s. They did so by taking two policy initiatives, both highly regressive, which resulted in bolstering food grains stocks with the Centre. Dr. Abhijit Sen's highly analytical Report on 'Long Term Grain Policy' (2002) provides interesting insights into this intriguing phenomenon. First, Government introduced in 1997, targeting the public distribution system (PDS). To quote from the Sen's Report: 'Thus, the narrow targeting of the PDS based on absolute income poverty is likely to have excluded a large part of the nutritionally vulnerable population from PDS' (GoI, 2002: 59). Second, cereal prices in real terms rose sharply during the 1990s: on wholesale price index (WPI) basis, real prices rose by

33.2 per cent between 1990-91 and 1999-2000 (Ibid.: 44). The issue prices of food grains distributed through PDS were raised continuously during this period, as a result of deliberate policy designed to cut down on food subsidy. In effect this meant 'exclusion' of the poorest sections of population who found that food grains became increasingly inaccessible. Both these policy initiatives of 'exclusion' were inspired by the Indian policymakers' obsession with cutting down the size of food subsidy, so that fiscal deficit could be contained. Indian policymakers of the 1990s were fond of repeating parrot-like the phrase borrowed from IMF/World Bank vocabulary: 'There is no free lunch'. As a cumulative result of these mindless measures, food grains stocks with the Centre reached an embarrassingly high level soaring at one point of time, to 60 million tonnes. Exports offered a soft option. Indian exports of rice and wheat during the three consecutive years 2001-02 to 2003-04 soared to a staggering figure of 27 million tonnes. The height of the irony was, these exports were subsidised. India is the abode of the largest number of underfed and chronically undernourished persons in the world and exports of food grains on such a massive scale is nothing short of development atrocity. Intellectual servility of Indian policymakers of the 1990s to the IMF/World Bank market theology thus spelt disaster to reduction of poverty or elimination of hunger objectives. In fact we should make a bonfire of that brand of development economics which only exhorts us to increase the production of food grains, without at the same time, providing a *modus operandi* by which food grains so produced reach the needy.

While on this subject, let us take the other two contradictions. We want to eliminate subsidies to domestic consumption of food grains with the ultimate objective of reducing fiscal deficit. Yet, we do not have any qualms about subsidising foreign consumers of India's food grains through export subsidies. This is more glaring because international prices of wheat and rice do not reflect market prices. The massive subsidies provided to agriculture by the US and the OECD countries are trade-distorting. In the WTO forum these countries have stubbornly refused to reduce their subsidies to agriculture and the negotiations have reached an impasse.

The other case relates to interest rates. The financial sector reforms introduced in the 1990s seem to have been designed to pamper the private corporate sector and the net result has been the emergence of an inequitable interest rate structure. For instance, while a high rated corporate could raise money from banks at 6 per cent, the small farmer continued to pay at a rate of 12 per cent. I have discussed this issue extensively in my previous book (Mujumdar, 2002). Here again, the intellectual servility of Indian policymakers of the 1990s to the market theology stands exposed. The ostensible reason for the farmer being made to pay a rate of interest higher than a corporate entity was that the 'risks' involved in 'agricultural business' are greater than those involved in corporate lending. This is what standard textbooks by economists from the developed economies expound. We must look at the problem from a broader perspective of the role of credit in a developing economy. In the Indian economy, credit has a dual role: growth-enhancing and risk reducing. Lending to agriculture, especially for purposes of reducing risks in agriculture like digging a well or a borewell, or even for rain water harvesting and conservation, should attract a concessional interest rate. Because, at the same time as such credit seeks to promote produciton, it also tends to reduce risks in the form of drought, etc. Viewed from this angle, it becomes clear that western textbook concept of risk is flawed. I have examined this issue thoroughly in the monograph prepared for NABARD (Mujumdar, 2005). Yet, nothing seems to have changed on that ground. The only consolation is that Reserve Bank of India (RBI) has at last conceded the point. Its Report on *Currency and Finance 2005-2006*, admits that, 'to compensate for sub-BPLR lending, other segments are charged higher rates of interest, thus leading to cross-subsidisation of the economically well-off borrowers by the economically poor borrowers' (RBI, 2006: 159). RBI needs to be congratulated on its open admission of misguided interest rate policy pursued in the 1990s. One hopes that this aspect of evolving an equitable interest structure will receive immediate attention of RBI, especially because of its critical importance to financial inclusion.

Contemporary Indian policymakers, including the framers of the Eleventh Plan should do a penance for yet another reason. It may be appropriate to refer here to the Global Hunger Index compiled recently by the International Food Policy Research Institute (IFPRI), Washington D.C. This index captures three dimensions of hunger: (i) availability of insufficient food in terms of quantity, (ii) shortfalls in nutritional status of children, and (iii) child mortality attributable to undernutrition. The index ranks countries on a 100-point scale, with 0 being the best score i.e., no hunger, and 100 being the worst, though neither of these extremes obtains in practice. In general, values greater than 10 indicate a serious problem, values greater than 20 fall in an 'alarming' category. India scores 25 and is worse off than Sri Lanka, Pakistan and Nepal (See Weismann, 2006).

Against this background, export of food grains on a massive scale and charging interest rates to agriculture on the so-called 'risk' basis, merely reflect the mindless pursuit of market theology, and an amateurish understanding of basic development issues.

One more example of how wisdom has at last dawned on the mainstream development economics can be found in the area of water. Traditionally, World Bank has been advocating privatisation and pricing of water as a solution to water scarcity. Empirical experience has shown that 'water pricing operates on the perverse principle that poorer you are the more it costs', (See Davis and Manuel, 2006). The poorest households of EL Salvador, Nicaragua and Jamaica devote more than 10 per cent of their income on water. In the United Kingdom, by contrast, spending more than 3 per cent of family earnings on water bills is considered an economic hardship. Development discourse has finally emerged out of this dead-end debate on privatisation and pricing of water. The *Human Development Report 2006*, referred to above, advocates that access to safe and affordable water supply should be considered a basic human right. Governments should therefore ensure that all citizens have access to a minimum of 20 litres of clean water per day, and that those who cannot afford to pay get it for free. This should be a lesson for those Indian policymakers who fervently believe in the received doctrine of 'there is no free lunch'.

Does our Approach Paper to the Eleventh Plan reflect this new-found concern for 'inclusive growth' in the mainstream development economics? Or, could we not regard this as only a new label to the old-fashioned concept of 'broad-based and decentralised growth', which some of us have been advocating for many years? One thing is quite certain. In the present Indian context inclusive growth has become both a growth and development imperative: growth, because a high GDP growth like 8 or 9 per cent can be sustained in the medium term only if other sectors or segments of the economy, which have been sluggish because of a number of factors including policy neglect, can be activated. Development, because this is perhaps, the best route by which the bulk of the poor can be provided with livelihood and food security.

'Inclusiveness' may be said to have two dimensions: one, in terms of sectors or segments of the economy which need to be brought into the fold of a vibrant economy; and two, in terms of enabling sections of the population, whom the growth process has bypassed, to fully engage themselves with the development process.

Contemporary experience of China is illuminating in this context. It was the vibrant rural non-farm sector which played a critical role in the success story of drastically reducing poverty and unemployment. China's township and village enterprises (TVEs) provided increasing job opportunities outside agriculture thereby augmenting sources of household income. The phenomenal growth of this sector is demonstrated by the fact that its contribution of GDP rose to nearly one-third of total GDP in 2004, from practically zero in 1952.

All those involved in the development of the Indian economy—banks, cooperatives, development finance institutions, NGOs, and administrators—will have to re-think their own strategies in response to the new emphasis being given on 'inclusive growth'. Perhaps, the first step in this direction is to identify the segments of the rural economy, on the analogy of the Chinese experience, which have so far not attracted adequate attention by policymakers but which have the potential for robust growth. The loan portfolios of banks and other rural lending institutions must begin to reflect the more diversified credit support to these emerging segments.

Facilitating inclusive growth is a far more complicated process, involving micro planning, evolving area specific solutions, and participation of a number of actors—panchayati raj institutions, Central and state governments, NGOs, SHGs, etc. Inclusive growth also demands a committed bureaucracy and more imaginative policymakers, from both of whom a proactive role is warranted. One hopes, equal attention will be paid to building up these capabilities.

References

Davis, Kemal and Trewor Manuel (2006). "Not a Drop to Drink", *Times of India*, November 15.

Mujumdar, N.A. (2004). *Economic Reforms Sans Development*. New Delhi: Academic Foundation.

———. (2002). *Financial Sector Reforms and India's Economic Development* (Two Volumes), New Delhi: Academic Foundation.

———. (2005). "Risk Philosophy: An Enquiry into Risks and Uncertainties in Agriculture and the Role of Credit", *Occassional Paper* No. 41. Mumbai: NABARD.

Planning Commission (2006). *Towards Faster and More Inclusive Growth: An Approach to the 11th Five Year Plan*. New Delhi: Planning Commission. p.1.

Weismann, Doris (2006). *2006 Global Hunger Index: A Basis for Cross-Country Comparisons*.

Edited version of the Special Lecture delivered at the Mahatma Gandhi Department of Rural Studies, Veer Narmada South Gujarat University, Surat, March 26, 2007.

2 Native Discourse on Development

Is the Indian economy in the pink of its health today? Apparently, the answer would be an unhesitating 'yes', judged by the usual indicators of GDP growth, savings and investment, export growth, inflow of foreign direct investment (FDI) and appreciation of the Indian rupee. According to UNCTAD World Investment Report, India has emerged in 2007 as the second most attractive destination, after China, for global FDI. All this has led to uncritical celebration of the post-reform development model as a success story of a market-driven economy. A deeper probe into the growth process, however, reveals that all is not well with the Indian economy.

A community-centred analysis reveals that there is large-scale unemployment, both among the educated and the uneducated, the incidence of hunger and malnutrition continues to remain at an alarmingly high level. The interest rate structure has become inequitable: the private corporate sector is pampered and the small borrower is discriminated against. It is a case of economically weak borrowers subsidising strong borrowers. The phenomenon of farmers suicides has spread widely. The insensitiveness with which the authorities have gone about in widespread acquisition of arable land for special economic zones (SEZs) is sometimes appalling. There is alienation of land from tribals, though the legislation to confer land rights on tribals is in place. The reform-obsessed mindset of the policymakers has thus become the stumbling block for development.

Analytically, it is convenient to divide the post-reform period into two distinct phases: the first phase beginning from 1991 when major economic reforms of liberalisation of the Indian economy were introduced up to 2004. The period subsequent to 2004 forms the second phase. While the first phase can be broadly categorised as 'era of exclusion', the second phase constitutes the era of 'inclusive growth'. The first phase witnessed the mindless pursuit of 'growth only' policies inspired by the market theology of the IMF and World Bank. No doubt there was acceleration of GDP growth but this was accompanied by growing unemployment and increasing impoverishment of the poor, as mentioned earlier.

Fortunately, Indian policymakers realised, though belatedly, their mistakes in terms of distorted priorities like total neglect of agriculture. In 2004, they announced the target of doubling the quantum of credit flowing to agriculture in the subsequent three years. Thus the year 2004 marks a watershed. In the post-2004 phase we also see the emergence of the National Rural Employment Guarantee Scheme—the best that could have happened to the rural poor. The scheme, which is a demand-driven scheme, carrying a legal guarantee for employment was launched in February 2006, covering initially 200 districts. It has recently been extended to all districts.

The policymakers have now realised that future agricultural growth would be water-centric. A National Rainfed Area Authority (NRAA) was established in November 2006 to support upgradation and management of dryland and rainfed agriculture. It would coordinate all schemes relating to watershed development. The Union Budget 2007-08 provides 100 per cent subsidy to small and marginal farmers, and 50 per cent subsidy to other farmers to erect structures, which would divert rain water into dug wells. The Accelerated Irrigation Benefit Programme (AIBP) has also been streamlined. The Bharat Nirman Programme envisages creation of 10 million hectares of additional assured irrigation during the four years 2005-2009. Thus irrigation has been brought back to its central position.

The Reserve Bank of India (RBI), on its part, began to initiate measures to promote financial inclusion designed to bring the bulk of the rural population into the fold of modern banking system. At present almost 40 per cent of the adult population of the country comprising mainly those living on low incomes and those without collateral is unable to access mainstream financial products. A number of steps have been taken to facilitate financial inclusion: banks opening 'no frills account' with low charges, banks 'appointing business facilitators' or 'business correspondents' to reach customers, and so on. The broad idea is that at least one district in each state should be targeted for 100 per cent financial inclusion. A Financial Inclusion Fund (FIF) is being established with NABARD for meeting the cost of developmental and promotional interventions. Already 100 per cent financial inclusion has been achieved in 28 districts and in Puducherry. It should therefore be possible to achieve enhanced and easy access to institutional credit. It is perhaps the search for an alternative paradigm of growth, which has led the policymakers, in the post-2004 phase, to 'inclusive growth' which is pro-poor and which may provide answers to dilemmas faced by the market-driven approach to development in the first phase. The title of the Eleventh Plan—'Towards Faster and More Inclusive Growth' (2006) reflects this fundamental transformation of our approach to development. In fact we may construe the resort to inclusive growth as a sort of penance that policymakers have now chosen for the atonement of sins they committed in the first phase in mindless pursuit of market theology. In a way inclusive growth is only a new label to the rather old-fashioned concept of 'broad-based and decentralised growth' which some of us have been advocating for many years. The point to be driven home is that we have now discovered the native discourse on development, as contra-distinguished from received wisdom or imported growth models. This native discourse is designed to tackle India specific issues, rather than chasing issues described in textbooks on development based on market theology.

Let us begin with some basic facts. Taking the Tenth Five-Year Plan (2002-03 to 2006-07) as a whole, real GDP growth works out to 7.6 per cent per annum—the fastest growth in any Plan period, and significantly higher than 5.7 per cent growth recorded during the 1980s and the 1990s. Per capita income grew by 6.1 per cent per annum in the Tenth Plan, and what is more, by 7.1 per cent during the last four years (2003-04 to 2006-2007). This rate is more than double the rate of 3.4 per cent increase witnessed in the 1980s and 1990s.

Domestic savings and investment rates reached record highs during 2005-06. Gross domestic savings rose to 32.4 per cent of GDP in 2005-06 from 31.1 per cent in 2004-05 and 23.5 per cent in 2001-02. India thus ranks among the high saving economies.

India's exports growth has been sustained at around 23 per cent in both 2005-06 and 2006-07. The ratio of merchandise exports to GDP has been rising since 1990s, reflecting India's growing international competitiveness.

Net capital flows to India remained buoyant in 2006-07 at $45 billion or 4.9 per cent of GDP and exceeding the current account deficit. Higher capital flows could be attributed to the strengthening of macroeconomic fundamentals, greater investor confidence and surfeit of global liquidity. Net FDI inflows into India increased sharply from US $7.7 billion in 2005-2006 to US $19.4 billion during 2006-07. In the current financial year, up to early October 2007, the foreign exchange reserves of RBI rose by over US $50 billion and this unprecedented flood of inflow of capital has posed serious challenges for both monetary management and the capital market. The Prime Minister's Economic Advisory Council has estimated that an increase in the forex reserves of RBI of US $26 billion in 2007-08 would be consistent with current real growth of the economy, say, 8.5 or 9 per cent moderate monetary expansion (17.5 per cent) and a tolerable inflation rate (4 per cent). Already, we have exceeded the limit. These inflows, are playing havoc in the stock market with the Sensex moving to new heights well above 19,000 and showing a greater degree of volatility.

These are indeed achievements which the reformers may claim are attributable to reforms. But we cannot push below the carpet the pitfalls of reforms. During the first phase of reforms, the policy focus was on liberalisation, market-led growth, fiscal correction, promotion of private and foreign investment developments of the capital market, creation of an environment of consumerism. In the euphoria of these glamorous reforms, more basic issues were overlooked resulting in what could be called an 'era of exclusion'. A large number of small farmers were pushed out of commercial banks loan-portfolio. Similarly, a sizeable number of poor families were thrown out of the public distribution system (PDS). The less glamorous sectors like agriculture were neglected. No wonder agricultural growth decelerated from 3.1 per cent during the 1990s to 2.2 per cent during the Tenth Plan period. The deceleration in agricultural growth could be attributed to declining public investment in agriculture and reduced flow of credit to agriculture. Public investment in agriculture declined from 3.4 per cent of agricultural GDP during 1976-1980 to 2.6 per cent in 2005-06. The rural credit delivery system was allowed to become moribund. The addition to the irrigation potential during the Tenth Plan was 8.8 million hectares; this was only one-half of the target. In fact there was no increase in the actual irrigated area during the Tenth Plan.

Edited version of the lecture delivered at the Seminar organised in memory of Dr. I.G. Patel by the Gujarat Economic Association, Baroda, October 27, 2007.

3 Contemporary Relevance of Mahatma Gandhi's Economic Philosophy

Mahatma Gandhi started the Satyagraha movement—'the firmness of the force of truth'—on 11th September 1906 and to commemorate the centenary of the movement, the Indian National Congress convened an international conference on 'Peace, Non-Violence and Empowerment: Gandhian Philosophy in the 21st Century', in New Delhi on 29-30 January 2007. That the appeal of the Mahatma is universal is reflected in the fact that delegates from 91 countries and 129 organisations participated in the conference; countries included, small and big, developed and developing, and countries from the former communist block (Sharma, 2007). It is indeed an intellectual treat to browse through this carefully edited volume and no social scientist can afford to miss this book. It transports us to an altogether different world from the usual dry and doctrinaire discourses on development.

The volume is divided into five sections: Section I—Gandhian Philosophy in the 21st century; Section II—A Non-violent Approach to Conflict Resolution and Peace Building; Section III—Gandhian Philosophy for Poverty Eradication, Education and People's Empowerment; Section IV—Dialogue among Peoples and Cultures; and Section V—Towards a Nuclear Weapons-free and Non-violent World Order.

The theme of the conference was is so eclectic that, obviously it would not be possible to do justice to it if we attempt to cover the whole subject in this brief review. Instead, the review seeks to focus on poverty and related economic issues. A distinguished participant in the conference emphasises: 'I am struck by the enormous range of relevance that Gandhi's life as well as his writings have for us in the political world today' (Sharma, 2007: 105); and one would like to add 'economic world'. In a way, the whole attempt of the conference was, as C.K. Prahalad puts it appropriately, to 'recontextualise Gandhi for the 21st Century' (Ibid.: 155).

The uniqueness of the Mahatma was that not only was he obsessed with the objective of eradicating poverty but also that he opted voluntarily to live poverty, as it were. To quote Rabindranath Tagore: 'He stopped at the threshold of huts of the thousands of dispossessed, dressed like one of their own. He spoke to them in their own language. Here was living truth at last, and not only quotation from books. For this reason the Mahatma, the name given to him by the people of India, is his real name' (Ibid.: 185). Perhaps this experience enabled him to view poverty in a macro socio-economic perspective, instead of treating it as merely statistics of assessing the number of people below the poverty line (BPL), as we are now accustomed. Bhikhu Parekh has admirably encapsulated the poverty profile, as sketched by the Mahatma, in the following paragraph:

> Second, poverty dehumanises human beings, wastes the potential and deprives their lives of all sense of meaning and purpose. It is one of the worst forms of violence that human beings can commit against other human beings. It is as bad as killing, and even worse for the fact that it is silent, slow and invisible, arouses no anger, and is outside the purview of anyone's direct responsibility. As long as even one person is starved, is malnourished or lacks decent housing, the social order stands indicted lacking legitimacy. Basic human needs have the first claim on Society's resources, and it has an obligation to arrange its economic affairs in a manner that the needs of all its members are met (Ibid.: 140).

The guidelines for development policy formulation were given by the Mahatma himself: 'I will give you a talisman. Whenever you are in doubt, or when the self becomes too much with you, apply the following test. Recall the face of the poorest and the weakest man whom you may have seen, and ask yourself if the step you contemplate is going to be of any use to him. Will he gain anything by it? Will it restore to him a control over his own life and destiny? In other words, will it lead to Swaraj for the hungry and spiritually starving millions? Then you will find your doubts and your self melt away' (Statement made in August 1947, Ibid.: 141).

Judged by these twin criteria, how does our performance in the area of development fare? Far from satisfactory. To quote Prahalad again: 'Actually, today, in India, there are more poor people than the entire population of India in 1930. That is a reality that we have to confront' (Ibid.: 156). This is the situation after we have completed 10 five-year development plans! The policy environment seems to have particularly worsened since the 1990s, after the liberalisation of the Indian economy and the introduction of concomitant economic reforms. The policymakers seem to have shown neither the passion for reducing poverty nor the compassion to the poor. This is because one of the byproducts of reforms has been the intoxication of the Indian policymakers with the undiluted market theology of the IMF and the World Bank. One hopes that the present study will have a detoxifying effect on such policymakers.

Two examples can be cited in support of the above statement. First, in respect of food grains management policy, what is disturbing is that India which is the abode of the largest number of chronically underfed and undernourished persons in the world, exported a huge quantity of 27 million tonnes of food grains during the three consecutive years, 2001-02 to 2003-04 (Mujumdar, 2007: 95). This was the result of two regressive measures taken earlier: first, the Government introduced in 1997, targeting in the public distribution system (PDS) in the form of Targeted PDS or TPDS. 'Thus, the narrow targeting of the PDS based on absolute income poverty is likely to have excluded a large part of the nutritionally vulnerable population from the PDS.' Second, due to the continuous raising of the issue prices of food grains, the concessionally priced food grains became increasingly inaccessible to the poor. Cereal prices, in real terms, rose by 33.2 per cent between 1990-91 and 1999-2000. The inevitable consequence was the mounting food grains stocks with the Food Corporation of India (FCI). No wonder our policymakers saw a soft option in exports for tackling the issue of the so-called 'surplus food grains'. This was nothing short of development atrocity. The irony was further compounded: while our objective in taking the two regressive measures mentioned above was to reduce subsidies for domestic consumption of food grains, the same policymakers did not have any qualms about subsidising exports of our food grains! If the Mahatma were alive, perhaps, one could speculate, there would have been a *satyagraha* against such mindless pursuit of flawed food grains management policy.

The second example pertains to the current controversy surrounding special economic zones (SEZs). The insensitiveness with which farmers are being alienated from the lands they are cultivating, for establishing SEZs, is, at least in some cases, appalling. The Nandigram episode leaves a bitter taste in the mouth. Contrast this with the Mahatma's approach. When Birla set up a mill in the princely state of Gwalior, the government obtained the land for him without paying adequate compensation to its poor owners. Gandhi pursued the matter with him in a series of letters and told him to drop the project rather than harm the just and legitimate interests of the poor (Ibid.: 143). The present day policymakers would do well to carefully read this volume.

In the name of economic reforms, there were other policy mistakes committed: the flow of credit to agriculture declined sharply, a large number of small farmers were thrown out of the banking system and an inequitable interest rate structure biased against the small borrowers and in favour of the private corporate sector emerged.[1] The Reserve Bank of India (RBI, 2007) has recently conceded in its report that, 'to compensate for sub-BPLR lending, other segments are charged higher rates of interest, thus leading to cross subsidisation of the economically well-off borrowers by economically poor borrowers.'

While the record in the areas of food security, employment and financial engineering is quite disappointing, there is much to celebrate in terms of empowerment of the poor. Edward Samuel Miliband of Britain pays compliments to India for her progress in education and decentralisation of political power: 'We strongly admire the lead shown by India with Primary Education for All Programme—*Sarva Shiksha Abhiyan*' (Sharma, 2007: 170). He also makes a reference to programmes of educating of street children in metropolitan centres. But Marianne Mikko (former member of European Parliament) exhorts India to go a step forward: 'Finland has been emphasising technical education for some decades now. As a result, the majority of us present here today probably have Nokia cell phones in our pockets. Thinking ahead, even before the goals of *Sarva Shiksha Abhiyan* are achieved, new goals must be set. In most of Europe, only primary education is compulsory. But, most countries regard secondary education as a norm. I am sure India will also set this goal for itself. India should set itself a goal of letting the local talent to flourish so that they can rival any talent in the world' (Ibid.: 188).

1. For a fuller discussion see Sharma (2007).

Reverting to Miliband, 'I think what Gandhi taught us was that the extraordinary things could be achieved if the power is in the right hands. That is why India, I think, is to be congratulated on the integration of the *panchayat raj* system of local government in which there are now three million elected members and one million of them are women, I think this is the largest representation of women at elected level in the world' (Ibid.: 170).

Muhammad Yunus (Bangladeshi Economist) asserts that, 'Mahatma Gandhi's life and example have influenced not just the history of our subcontinent but indeed of the values of modern civilisation. At the United Nations, the world had united in the year 2000 to adopt the Millennium Development Goals which aimed to reduce extreme poverty by half before 2015' (Ibid.: 35). Yunus's main contribution is in the sphere of finance. He argues that the existing financial institutions have systematically excluded the poor from financial services and this amounts to financial apartheid. 'What the Grameen Bank has sought to do over the 30 years since its inception is to provide financial services to the very poor on terms that are suited to them' (Ibid.: 36). Microcredit has thus emerged as an important institution which contributes in a significant way to poverty reduction. Globally, nearly 100 million of the world's poorest have now been reached with microcredit. The recent emphasis that Indian policymakers have placed on expansion of microcredit institutions perhaps reflects a response to this movement.

Market phobia does not disappear so easily, however. One of the methods recommended by C.K. Prahalad for implementing Gandhi's message in the 21st century is: 'Allow the market to allocate resources in a transparent fashion such that resource-use is constrained. Eliminating energy subsidies, pricing water appropriately...' (Ibid.: 159). Lets take up the pricing of water issue. Traditionally, the World Bank has been advocating privatisation and pricing of water as a solution to water scarcity. It had to retreat from this position because empirical experience has shown that water pricing 'operates on the perverse principle that poorer you are the more it costs' (Davis and Manuel, 2006). The *Human Development Report 2006*, affirms that access to safe and affordable water supply should be considered as a basic human right. The government should, therefore ensure that all citizens have access to a minimum of 20 litres of clean water per day and those who cannot afford to pay get it free. In India, we should treat water security on par with food security. We need not be shy of subsidies because after all, subsidisation is a characteristic of a civilised society.[2]

Happily, on the eve of the Eleventh Plan all this is changing. Indian policymakers seem to have gone through a process of intellectual transformation to realise that moving away from undiluted market theology is essential to ensure that the development content of growth does not wither away. The Eleventh Plan itself is based on a strategy of inclusive growth in the real sector. Rural employment guarantee scheme is the best that could have happened to the rural poor. On its part, RBI is pursuing the policy of financial inclusion. Already, 100 per cent financial inclusion is achieved in 28 districts in 8 states and in Puducherry. Microcredit institutions are being actively promoted. The quantum of credit flow to agriculture doubled during the three-year period 2004-2007. While the change in the approach to development is in the right direction, we have a long way to go.

References

Davis, Kemul and Trewor Manuel (2006). "Not a Drop to Drink", *The Times of India*, November 15.

Government of India (2002). *Report of the High Level Committee on Long Term Grain Policy for the Country*, Chairman: Abhijit Sen. New Delhi. p.59.

Indian Journal of Agricultural Economics (2007). "Review of World Development Report, 2006", *Indian Journal of Agricultural Economics*, January-March 2007. p.155.

Mujumdar, N.A. (2007). "First Principles of Foodgrains Management", in *Inclusive Growth*. New Delhi: Academic Foundation. p.95.

Reserve Bank of India (2007). *Report on Currency and Finance, 2005-06.* p.159.

Sharma, Anand (ed.) (2007). *Gandhian Way: Peace, Non-Violence and Empowerment*. Indian National Congress. New Delhi: Academic Foundation. pp. 320.

2. Indian Journal of Agricultural Economics (2007).

4 Philosophy of Sustainable Development

There is a massive literature on sustainable development and the UN and related multilateral agencies dealing with trade, environment and poverty have made their own contribution to this growing literature. Prof. U. Sankar (2008) in his scholarly paper, has given a sample of the definitions of sustainable development. One of them is 'meeting the needs of the present generation without compromising the needs of future generations'. A more eclectic definition is by World Commission on Environment and Development (WCED, 1987): 'sustainable development is a process of change in which exploitation of resources, the direction of investments, the orientation of technological development and institutional change are all in harmony and enhance both the current and future potentials to meet human needs and aspiration'.

Here, I would not seek to discuss the nuances of these definitions but to provide you the broad canvass of what I would prefer to call the philosophy of sustainable development. I would submit that only against the background of such a broad canvas can a blueprint for sustainable development for a specific country can be worked out meaningfully.

The choice of the word 'philosophy' is deliberate. The parameters within which issue of sustainable development need to be addressed have witnessed a significant transformation. First, development economics has discarded the age-worn 'trickle-down' theory of growth and has embraced 'inclusive growth'. Second, the private sector is no longer guided by Milton Friedman's dictum: maximisation of profits is its sole objective. The 21st century model of a private company shows ample awareness of the larger concerns of the community, including depletion of natural resources and environmental degradation. Predatory capitalism is dead.

There are thus, three essential ingredients of the receipe for sustainable development. First, while most writers on sustainable development seem to emphasise inter-generational equity, intra-generational equity is equally important. The very survival of the community depends on how soon we would facilitate the attainment of intra-generational equity. Survival comes first before sustainability. Second, many writers seem to over-emphasise the role of public policy in sustainable development: The attainment of sustainable development is a cooperative enterprise in which both the private and public sectors have a role to play. Third, in both the cases, private and public community-centred development holds the key to attainment of sustainable development.

Intra-Generational Equity

Let us begin with our own experience of development. The Eleventh Five-Year Plan (2007-08 to 2011-12) aims at putting the economy in a sustainable growth trajectory with a growth rate of 10 per cent in the terminal year. Rapid growth is an essential part of strategy for growth and development but we have now realised that the growth process has by-passed certain sectors of the economy and sections of the population. Inclusive growth, or broad-based and decentralised growth, is therefore the new strategy adopted by the Eleventh Plan. Inclusive growth has become a growth and development imperative: growth because a high GDP growth can be sustained only if other sectors or segments of the economy, which have been sluggish because of a number of factors, including policy neglect, can be activated. Development, because this is perhaps the best route by which the bulk of the poor, whom the process of growth has bypassed, can be provided with livelihood and food security (Mujumdar, 2007a; 2007b).

This new-found concern for growth with equity shows that development economics has come a long way from its earlier position. In the early 1950s, when the Indian Planning Commission sought to build equity into the development plan, the mainstream development economists scoffed at the idea. Their dictum was: enlarge the size of the national cake: distribution will take care of itself. These were the hey-days of the percolation or trickle-down theory of growth—a theory which has been disproved by empirical experience. Equity is intrinsically important as a development goal in its own right. But sharing of economic and political opportunities is also instrumental for economic growth and development. In other words, equity reinforces the growth process itself. Promoting intra-generational equity has thus acquired a new dimension in strategies for sustainable developments.

Nearly 100 years ago, Mahatma Gandhi emphasised: 'Basic human needs have the first claim on Society's resources and it has an obligation to arrange its economic affairs in a manner that the needs of all its members are met'.[1] You cannot have little islands of affluence or opulence in an ocean of poverty. The social system to be sustainable has to first ensure that basic needs of all are met. The contemporary relevance of Gandhi's economic philosophy is quite remarkable. The community-centredness of the approach to sustainability is thus underlined.

Private Corporate Sector

In the current discussions on the so-called social responsibility of the private corporate sector, it is customary to assure that such responsibility is in the nature of glorified charity. It was left to the Coca-Cola Chief, Edward Neville Isdell, who represents the not so pretty face of modern capitalism, scarred as it is by the recent Enron and Enron-like episodes, to redefine corporate responsibility. As guest editor of the *Economic Times*, he wrote:

> The future of a 21st Century company is tied to the health of our communities and our planet. Some leaders may consider sustainability work to be in a company's "enlightened self-interest". I disagree. In ways that will determine our ability to achievc consistent, global growth and profitability it is quite literal self-interest.
>
> Editorial, March 17, 2008.

All researchers on sustainable development should sit up and take notice of this new 21st century corporate model for sustainability provided by Isdell. To explain briefly, water is the main ingredient in Coca-Cola; and lack of public access to clean water is a serious problem in many communities where Coca-Cola factories are functioning. Hence the objective of the Coca-Cola company has been to return water used in its manufacturing processes safely to the environment; the company supports more than 100 community water projects in 40 countries. In India the

1. See my review of the book: *Gandhian Way: Peace, Non-violence and Empowerment*, in *Indian Journal of Agricultural Economics*. October-December, 2007. p. 700.

company is installing more than 100 rain harvesting structures in 17 states.

This is in sharp contrast to the colonial regimes which facilitated rapacious exploitation of natural resources which benefited only the multinationals and the colonial powers leaving the community in the lurch. Copper mining in Zambia and gold mining in South Africa are instances in point.

To cite one more recent example, some multinational banks are making it clear to their borrowers that lending to industries with polluting technologies will attract higher rates of interest. This new awakening among the private corporate sector companies and financial institutions augurs well for sustainable development. Community-centredness has to be super-imposed on the private businesses.

I may add that even in today's India, some policymakers seem to have remained slaves to the ghosts of Milton Friedman, whom Isdell (2008) quotes:

> There is one and only social responsibility of business—to use its resources and engage in activities designed to increase its profits.

Let us hope that the Isdell model will help both the private sector and public policymakers to unlearn Friedman.

Empirical Experience

At this point it may be useful to raise the question: does the empirical experience of countries which have recorded sustained high growth in recent years—recent in the sense after the classic industrial revolution—offer any lessons for us? As we know, about a dozen economies, both large and medium size, witnessed an average GDP growth of 10 or nearly 10 per cent sustained over a decade (GoI, 2008). These include China, Singapore, Japan, Taiwan, Thailand, South Korea, Portugal, Greece and Hong Kong. Among these economies, four or five sustained growth of around 9 per cent for two decades or so. One of the critical elements in facilitating such sustained high growth was high investment in infrastructure. What is of paramount importance is the upgradation of infrastructure, both physical and social, particularly in power, roads and ports. A corrolary of this requirement is mobilisation of massive amounts of capital by both, private and public sectors.

Community-Centredness

Overall, it is clear that community-centredness holds the key to sustained development of the economy, whether we think in terms of public policy formulation or guidelines for functioning of private companies. Undiluted market theology, expounded by the IMF and the World Bank, which in the past has shaped policies in many developing countries, has thus to be tempered by this larger concern for the community as a whole.

References

Government of India (2008). *Economic Survey, 2007-08*, New Delhi, February. p. 18.

Mujumdar, N.A. (2007a). *Inclusive Growth: Development Perspectives in Indian Economy.*

———. (2007b). "Main-stream Development Economics and the Eleventh Plan", *Economic Developments in India* 116. New Delhi: Academic Foundation.

Sankar, U. (2008). "Environmentally Sound Technologies for Sustainable Development in India", Paper presented at the International Conference on *Issues in Public Policy for Sustainable Development*. IGNOU. 26 March.

World Commission on Environment and Development (WCED) (1987). *Our Common Future*. Oxford.

This is the edited version of the Keynote Address, given on 26th March, 2008 at the International Conference on *Issues in Public Policy and Sustainable Development*, organised by Indira Gandhi National Open University, New Delhi.

5 The Search for Elusive Growth

The Elusive Quest for Growth was the title of a book written in 2002 by William Easterly, a former World Bank economist. The same title perhaps remains appropriate for *The Growth Report: Strategies for Sustained Growth and Inclusive Development*, published by the World Bank in 2008, on behalf of the Commission on Growth and Development.

The publication in 1955 of the *Theory of Economic Growth* by Arther Lewis became a classic in what later emerged as the discipline of development economics. This pioneering work was regarded as belonging to the same genre as Adam Smith's *Wealth of Nations* (1776). Of course, growth is central to achieving a number of development objectives including poverty reduction. In the subsequent 55 years or so, we have built up a mountain of literature on growth and development contributed by academicians and official agencies like the World Bank and some UN agencies. One wonders whether we are any wiser today in terms of offering a workable blueprint of growth and development to a developing country, than what we were in the mid-1950s. But one thing is clear. As Peter de Haan (2006) puts it: 'The study of development economics provides the student with aesthetic pleasure. For instance, the neo-classical growth model and the subsequent improvements do indeed arouse aesthetic enthusiasm ...'. Haan doubts whether increasing sophistication of growth models and the emergence of a new breed of development workers linked to aid disbursement has contributed substantially 'to the promotion of growth and eradication of poverty in poor countries'.

No doubt these tomes of research and reports including the present *Growth Report* (World Bank, 2008), have facilitated a better understanding of the process of development. But this understanding has, alas, not led us to effectively tackle the problem of poverty. Erudition is no substitute for practical policy. In the final analysis, poverty and hunger are an affront to civilised society. How does one explain then, the alarming increase in hunger worldwide? FAO (2008) estimates that the number of undernourished at 923 million in 2007 was higher by 80 million than the figure in 1990-1992, the base period for the World Food Summit (WFS) hunger reduction target: 'This makes the task of bringing the number of undernourished to 420 million by 2015 more difficult especially in an environment of high food prices and uncertain global economic prospects'.

Furthermore, have the more recent events overtaken development economics? The collapse of the American capitalism in 2008 is as traumatic as the collapse of the communist Russia in 1991. It has changed dramatically the development policymaking landscape. Market fundamentalism based on the notion that markets are self-correcting, allocate resources efficiently and serve the public interest well has collapsed. The so-called 'Washington Consensus' in favour of privatisation, liberalisation and independent central bank focussing exclusively on a single point agenda of controlling inflation, now stands stripped off its sanctimonious robe.

The Commission on Growth and Development, sponsored by, among others, the World Bank started working on the theme in April 2006 and submitted its Report in June 2008. The Commission consisted of 19 well known leaders, mostly from developing countries, and experienced policy, government and business leaders. It included two Nobel Laureates in Economics—Robert Solow and Michael Spence and the latter chaired the Commission. From India, there is Montek Singh Ahluwalia. The Commission held 12 workshops on a wide range of policy issues relating to growth and development. More than 300 distinguished academicians presented papers at these workshops. Of course, the Report bears the imprint of the World Bank philosophy because Danny Leipziger of the World Bank was Vice Chair of the Commission, which was serviced by the World Bank staff.

In his Preface (World Bank, 2008: ix-x), the Chair Michael Spence claims: 'There is perhaps for the first time in history a reasonable chance of transforming the quality of life and creative opportunities for the vast majority of humanity. This report is an attempt to increase the likelihood that the hope becomes a reality'. Judging by the main recommendations emerging from the Report, this appears to be a tall claim. This is not to deny that the Report provides useful insights into the development process especially to Indian contemporary policymakers.

The Commission's main recommendations stem from an investigation into the empirical experiences of 13 economies which recorded an average annual GDP growth of 7 per cent for 25 years or longer, since 1950. These countries are: Botswana, Brazil, China, Hong Kong, Indonesia, Japan, The Republic of Korea, Malaysia, Malta, Oman, Singapore, Taiwan and Thailand. The Commission adds that two other countries, India and Vietnam are on their way to joining this group.

These success stories demonstrate that fast and sustained growth is possible. At this pace of expansion, an economy almost doubles in size every decade. The Commission rejects the view that these are 'economic miracles'. When Japan grew at this pace, some critics dubbed it as a special case propelled by post-war recovery. When the four East Asian tigers—Hong Kong, Taiwan, Singapore and Korea matched it, some critics said that it was possible because they were so small. When China surpassed them, critics said that it was only possible because China was so big. The Commission believes that there are perfectly rational explanations for these success stories.

Distilling the empirical experiences of these 13 countries, the Commission comes up with these five essential ingredients for fast and sustained growth: (i) these countries fully exploited the world economy; (ii) they maintained macroeconomic stability; (iii) they mustered high rates of saving and investment; (iv) they let markets allocate resources; and (v) they had committed, credible and capable governments.

So far so good. Can these ingredients help us to draw up blueprints for growth and development of other poor countries?: 'But it is hard to know how to replicate these characteristics' (World Bank, 2008: 28). That is the tragedy of development economics.

The Commission admits that there is no generic formula for growth. 'Each country has specific characteristics and historical experiences that must be reflected in its growth story' (World Bank, 2008: 2). Indian policymakers in the post-1990s phase were soaked in the market theology of IMF/World Bank and tried to mimic the American capitalist model. This was reflected in some financial sector reforms and in the obsession with privatisation. The Commission itself cautions that: 'Governments in the high-growth economies were *not* free-market purists' (Ibid.: 7; emphasis added). Both the high profile reformers, whether it is the Narasimham Committee which submitted its Report in 1998 or the Raghuram Rajan Committee of 2008, advocate privatisation of public sector banks. In the global financial conflagration, when the major private sector icons of commercial banks, investment banks, mortgage houses and insurance giants collapsed like a pack of cards, both in America and Europe, the Indian financial system, dominated by public sector, stood rock-like, unharmed. It is to the credit of Indian public sector banks that they have been able to blend successfully the objectives of social banking with the market philosophy of optimising profitability.

Take another example of our overzealous attempt, in the post-1990s phase, to propitiate foreign capital, both in terms of foreign direct investment (FDI) and portfolio investment. The Growth Commission is categorical on the issue: 'But capital inflows over the past several decades have a mixed record. Our view is that foreign Saving is an imperfect substitute for domestic saving, including public saving, to finance the investment a booming economy requires' (Ibid.: 3). If India's growth story continues to be intact, despite the global financial mess, it is because India has emerged as a high saving economy with gross domestic savings of 34 per cent of GDP. Investment as a per cent of GDP increased from 25 per cent in 2002-03 to 38 per cent in 2007-08. Of this, 13 percentage points increase as much as 10 percentage points was financed domestically through higher household, private sector and corporate savings. It is high time that contemporary policymakers begin paying greater attention to raise domestic savings.

Some market theologists, including the World Bank, have been highly critical of the employment provided under the National Rural Employment Guarantee Act. The World Bank Report, 2008 provides the rationale for such schemes—'governments should also establish social safety nets—which provide a source of income to people between jobs—and ensure uninterrupted access to basic services. These policies are both ethical and practical. Without them popular support for a growth strategy will quickly erode' (Ibid.: 6).

On the whole, the Report provides useful insights into formulating appropriate development policies.

This is a defining moment in the history of world economic thought. In more recent years, the Indian policymakers were soaked in the market theology of the World Bank and IMF, and there was the danger that they could become 'free market purists'. This is reflected particularly in the proposals, for financial sector reforms. Now there is a need for introspection on the part of contemporary Indian policymakers. Both the lessons derived from the collapse of the American capitalist system and the useful insights into the process of growth provided by this World Bank report should assist policymakers in their process of introspection.

References

FAO (2008). *The State of Food Insecurity in the World.*

Haan, Peter de (2006). *Development in Hindsight*. Amsterdam: KIT Publishers. p.10.

World Bank (2008). *The Growth Report: Strategies for Sustained Growth and Inclusive Development*. Washington D.C.: Commission on Growth and Development.

6 Growth, Natural Resources and Rural Livelihoods

The central theme of the course 'Management of Natural Resources for Sustainable Livelihoods for the Poor' is of great contemporary relevance for development economics itself. I would seek to provide a macro perspective of the whole range of issues involved. The kind of excessive pressure exerted by the rural poor on the natural resources for eking out a livelihood, as we witness it in the Indian economy today, is rather a unique phenomenon. Empirical experience of the developed countries clearly shows that as the process of industrialisation gathers momentum, the surplus population gets siphoned off from the rural sector to the non-farm sector. As a corrollary, this phenomenon reduces the pressure of rural population on natural resources. Even the contemporary experience of China is illuminating in this context. It was the vibrant rural non-farm sector which played a critical role in the success story of drastically reducing the levels of poverty and unemployment. China's township and village enterprises (TVEs) provided increasing job opportunities outside agriculture, thereby reducing the pressure on land. We are unable to replicate this sort of experience in India and hence we have to seek a 'second best' solution. Obviously, there are serious limitations on enlarging the quantum of resources like land; hence, the focus of policy will have to be perforce on enlarging the potential of natural resources for creating more avenues for livelihood through technological ingenuity, and through promotion of higher resource use efficiency.

Let me elaborate. Although India has entered, in recent years, into the league of fastest-growing economies—for instance, the average annual GDP growth rate was around 8 or 9 per cent during the last five years—the phantom of poverty continues to stare in our face. No doubt the percentage of population below the poverty line (BPL) declined from 36 per cent in the 1990s to around 27 per cent in mid-2000s. But in terms of absolute numbers, the problem remains formidable. Out of about 30 crore of BPL persons, around 22 crore persons or 73 per cent of the total poor live in rural areas. In other words, a staggering figure of 4.5 crore of BPL families in the rural sector pose a serious challenge. In addition to size, there is another dimension to their poverty. Although agriculture's contribution to GDP has declined over the years from some 50 per cent to 18 per cent, reflecting the process of industrialisation, the dependence on agriculture has not declined. Over 60 per cent of the population continues to depend on agriculture for its livelihood which implies heavy dependence on livelihoods on natural resources mainly land, water and forests. It is this combination of large size and excessive dependence on natural resources for livelihood which constitutes the core of the problem of more efficient utilisation of natural resources.

In the ultimate analysis, the overall growth of GDP sets the tone for sustaining or even enlarging rural livelihoods. This is because of the forward and backward linkages that agriculture has with the rest of the economy. This is true of agricultural growth also; the higher the growth in the agricultural sector, the greater the scope for employment in the rural sector. Rainfed areas in the country account for 60 per cent of the cultivated area and are home to the bulk of the poor. Agricultural development in future will have to be therefore, necessarily water-centric. Five inter-connected programmes assume significance in this context: watershed development programmes both micro and macro; rainwater harvesting and conservation; renovation of traditional water bodies; improving water use efficiency in public irrigation works, notably in canals; and promotion of micro-irrigation technology like drip and sprinkler irrigation systems. Of all these, I have called watershed development the mother of all water management modes (Mujumdar, 2007).

The point is that the scope for increasing the size of culturable land is practically nil; so also there is no known technology for increasing the rainfall in dry regions. The solution therefore lies in the increasing resource use efficiency. The set of five inter-connected schemes for augmenting water supply referred to earlier, are an attempt in this direction.

Take another case of technology. The recent breakthrough in rice cultivation technology, known as sustainable rice intensification (SRI) in which synergic interaction increases use efficiency of land, labour and water is a case in point. It is actually land, water and seed saving technology (Swaminathan, 2008).

Dr. M.S. Swaminathan now talks about herbal biovalley: 'The goal of Biovalley is to promote biohappiness among tribal families through integrated attention the conservation, sustainable use and equitable use and equitable sharing of bioresources of the area leading to health, work and income security. Conservation Farming will include steps for soil health enhancement, harvesting and efficient use of rain water and saving and using plants for saving lives and strengthening livelihoods.' (Ibid.) He believes that biomass is an underutilised resource which could be utilised for enhancing income, energy and work security. We have technologies for waste utilisation and vermicomposting.

Forests are another natural resource on which the poor are heavily dependent. Under the policy initiative of joint forest management (JFM), degraded national forests have been handed over to the forest protection committees (FPCs) as community forests under a community-based property rights regime. In response to the National Forest Policy, the state governments have started encouraging the communities living nearby state forests for formation of forest protection group. There seems to be enormous scope for enlarging the avenues of rural livelihoods through the development and exploitation of forest products. For instance, a recent study of International Network for Bamboo and Rattan (INBAR) has shown that the market potential of bamboo and bamboo products from Orissa can be raised from the present level of Rs. 165 crore to over Rs. 600 crore per annum (Economic Times, 2006). Tribal communities are involved in bamboo plantation and primary processing of bamboo and hence, the enlargement of bamboo industry would add greatly to their livelihoods and incomes. Bamboo has multiple uses, including as food; the fresh young shoots procured by the tribals are also used as food.

Non-Farm Employment

A host of other employment avenues not strictly related to farm, can be thought of: development of wastelands, soil conservation, drainage and flood control, composit preparation, food processing, storage, marketing, aquaculture and floriculture.

The best thing that could have happened to the rural poor is the National Rural Employment Guarantee Act (NREGA) enacted in 2005. The Act guarantees 100 days of wage employment in a year to a rural household whose adult members are willing to do manual work. Under this scheme, various types of activities including water harvesting structures, drought proofing, minor and micro-irrigation works are undertaken. In 2007-08, 3.39 crore households benefited from the scheme (GoI, 2008).

If the labour employed under the scheme could be utilised to increase the efficiency of natural resource use, as discussed earlier, it would go some way towards enlarging rural livelihoods.

Philosophy of Sustainable Development

Finally, the objective of sustainability of livelihoods for the rural poor forms part of the broader philosophy of sustainable development. The latter is an amalgam of three ingredients—growth, ecological stability and inter-generational and intra-generational equity (Mujumdar, 2008).

The measures we have discussed for improving resource use efficiency are consistent with this broader objective of sustainable development.

References

Economic Times (2006). "Orissa can make Rs. 600 crore from Bamboo Trade", January 16.

GoI (2008). *Poverty Eradication in India by 2015*. Ministry of Rural Development, November 15.

Mujumdar, N.A. (2007). *Inclusive Growth: Development Perspectives in Indian Economy*. New Delhi: Academic Foundation.

———. (2008). "Philosophy of Sustainable Development", in *Economic Developments in India* 124. New Delhi: Academic Foundation.

Swaminathan, M.S. (2008). "Strengthening Food Security Based on Home Grown Food", Inaugural Address at 68th Annual Conference of *Indian Society of Agricultural Economics*. Visakhapatnam, November 28.

This is the edited version of the lecture, given on February 6, 2008, at the National Institute of Rural Development, Hyderabad.

7 Journey towards Holistic Development

From Milton Friedman to Mahatma Gandhi

The dimensions of development economics, it seems, keep on extending, over time. It may be recalled that in the early 1950s, when India's Planning Commission sought to build equity into the growth Plan, the mainstream development economists scoffed at the idea. Their dictum was: 'Enlarge the size of the national cake, the distribution would take care of itself'. Those were the hey-days of the percolation or trickle-down theory growth—a theory which has been disproved by empirical experience. Equity is intrinsically important as a development goal in its own right. But sharing of economic and political opportunities is also instrumental for economic growth and development. In other words, equity reinforces the growth process itself. This relatively new-found concern for growth with equity shows that development economics has come a long way. Was this belated recognition responsible for breeding predatory capitalism in the meanwhile? We are not sure. What we are sure is that the collapse of the American capitalist model in 2008 now warrants that we move away from predatory capitalism to what can be broadly described as community-centred capitalism.[1] Shedding our self-centredness, we must begin to sensitise ourselves not only to the woes of our less endowed brethren but also larger concerns, at the macro level, of depletion of natural resources, environmental degradation and inter-generational equity. This is what Mahatma Gandhi taught us nearly hundred years ago, by providing the philosophical basis for evolving a society with a value system which

---

1. For an in-depth discussion of the theme, you may see the following three articles by the author: "Native Discourse on Development"; "Philosophy of Sustained Development" and "Predatory Capitalism is Dead: Long Live Community-Centered Captialism", in *Economic Developments in India* 119, 124 and 132. New Delhi: Academic Foundation.

resonates to these larger concerns. In a broader context, the recent Commission on Growth and Development (World Bank, 2008) asserts that there is no generic formula for growth: 'Each country has specific characteristics and historical experiences that must be reflected in its growth strategy.' Is development economics moving away from a narrow mechanistic view of growth which has resulted in dubbing economics as a 'dismal science' to holistic development? Examining the more recent development experience of India, the reform phase beginning from 1991 when the liberalisation of the economy was initiated, to 2004 was the most retrogressive phase, battered as the economy was by the market theology obsessed reforms. The second phase subsequent to 2004 marks a gradual return to what one might call holistic development. We begin to wonder whether our contemporary policymakers have slowly begun to rediscover the Mahatma. The journey of the Indian economy from the Milton Friedman phase (1991-2004) to Mahatma Gandhi phase (2004-2009) needs to be authentically documented.

Collapse of the American Model

We are at a defining moment in the history of global economic system. The collapse of the capitalist model of the American economy in 2008 was as traumatic as the collapse of the communist model of Russia in 1991. Perhaps more traumatic because the US's 'economic crisis of historic proportions', to use the words of President Barack Obama, culminated in world recession. We have thus arrived at a moment in world economic history, when the disillusionment with the centrally planned economies is matched by the loss of faith in the capitalist system led by unbridled market forces. We have discarded the centrally planned economic system and if we now disown the capitalist system, where do we go from here? The present global economic crisis is ferocious and it has changed dramatically the institutional and policymaking landscape.

We may not have our own Reagonomics or Thatcherism to bury, but our contemporary policymakers are soaked in the market theology of IMF/ World Bank. It would not be easy to disengage them from the trappings of market theology and induce them to refrain from mimicking the Western models. The period of economic reforms—a period of liberalisation of the

Indian economy, from 1991 to 2004, was the most retrogressive phase in the history of India's economic development.

Retrogressive Phase: 1991-2004

Admittedly, India's growth story is impressive with GDP growth recording an annual average growth of 8.5 per cent during the last five years 2003 to 2008. In the euphoria of sustained high growth, we generally tend to overlook the mistakes committed by our policymakers during this phase. A community-centred analysis exposes clearly the darker side of these developments. While there is enough literature on the harm inflicted on the economy by the centrally planned economic phase—the so-called licence-permit-raj—little attention has been paid to the negative impact of the pursuit of unbridled market philosophy during the 1991-2004 phase. Economic historians need to pay greater attention to this phase.

I have characterised this period broadly as the Milton Friedman phase: Milton who is the principal protagonist of the so-called Chicago School, which expounds free markets, deregulation, liberalisation and globalisation. It advocates that the role of the state should be reduced to the minimum. As illustrative of this approach, look at Milton's corporate philosophy: 'There is one and only social responsibility of business—to use its resources and engage in activities designed to increase its profits'. Market fundamentalism embodied in the neoliberalism based on the notion that markets are self-correcting, allocate resources efficiently and serve the public interest well, has collapsed. It has now become clear that unbridled market forces are not self-correcting; regulation and direction of some sort is needed. The state has a critical role to play in the management of the economy.

During the first phase of reforms in India, our policymakers were soaked in this market theology. The focus was on liberalisation, market-led growth, fiscal correction, promotion of private and foreign investment, development of capital market and generally creation of an environment of consumerism. More basic issues of development were overlooked, which led to neglect of agriculture, deceleration of public investment in agriculture and in the flow of credit to agriculture, disdain for subsidies, whether food subsidy or credit subsidy, focussing on jobless growth, and disregard for the elementary principles of food security. I have extensively documented the pitfalls of these reforms elsewhere (Mujumdar, 2004a).

The 'growth culture' itself seems to have gone through a fundamental change during this phase, with reformers fond of repeating parrot-like phrases borrowed from IMF/World Bank vocabulary: 'There is no free lunch', perhaps meaning thereby that the poor must fend for themselves. The policymakers quoted with glee the American management guru James Goldsmith's well-known phrase: 'If you pay peanuts, you only get monkeys' (FAO, 2008). It required the collapse of the American financial icons—banks, insurance giants and mortgage houses in 2008 to realise that 'even if you pay cashew nuts, you get worse monkeys'. Chief executive officers (CEOs) of private corporate sector would say: 'We have money: we have a right to splurge'. Cumulatively, we appear to have sponsored sections of society, to borrow the expressive phrase of Arindam Chaudhuri, of 'dehumanised materialistic consumer dust bins'. The insensitiveness with which some state governments went about acquiring arable land, wrenching the small farmers from the land from which they were eking out their livelihood, for accommodating industries in the special economic zones (SEZs) was appalling. 'Industrialisation is what matters', the authorities seemed to argue. India, despite graduating to the league of fast growing economics in the world—even during the current world recession—continues to be the abode of the largest number of underfed and undernourished persons in the world. Recent FAO estimates show that the number of undernourished people in India has risen from 206 million in 1990-1992 to 230.5 million in 2003-2005, an increase of some 24 million (FAO, 2008). But our reformers gloat over the fact that in the liberalised Indian economy today, consumers can have the benefit of apples imported from Australia/New Zealand, grapes/oranges imported from USA and dog food from France.

I would be content with citing four concrete instances to substantiate how the mindless pursuit of market theology during the phase led to de-emphasise development: food grains management policy, inequitable rate regime, fiscal inequity and import of gold.

Food Grains Management Policy

As already discussed in respect of food grains management policy, what is disturbing is that India exported a huge quantity of 27 million tonnes of rice and wheat during the three consecutive years 2001-02 to 2003-04. This was the result of two regressive measures taken earlier: first, the Government introduces in 1997, targeting in the public distribution system (PDS) in the form of Targeted or TPDS. This narrow targeting of the PDS based on absolute income poverty excluded a large part of nutritionally vulnerable population from PDS. Second, due to the continuous raising of the issue price of food grains, the concessionally priced food grains became increasingly inaccessible to the poor. The inevitable consequence was the mounting food grains stocks with the Food Corporation of India (FCI). At one time, the stocks reached a peak of 60 million tonnes. No wonder, our policymakers sought a soft option in exports for tacking the issue of the so-called 'surplus food grains' (Mujumdar, 2007).

In my Introduction to a book on agriculture (Mujumdar and Kapila, 2007):

> It was tragic enough for a predominantly agricultural economy not to be able to produce in the 1960s adequate quantities of food grains to meet the domestic consumption requirements of the population: it is perhaps a greater systemic tragedy today that even when we are able to produce adequate quantities of food grains we are unable to ensure that food grains so produced do reach the needy.

Hunger and poverty are an affront to civilised society and subsidies are a characteristic of the civilised society. One begins to wonder whether we are dismissing poverty or reduction of poverty as mere phrases of a dialectic process, denying thereby its moral urgency of addressing the task.

Inequitable Interest Rate Regime

Those who pontificate on why the concessional lending rates do not help the poor, further expose their innocence of the realities of the present interest rate structure. As already discussed financial sector and banking sector reforms implemented in the 1990s have resulted in the emergence of an inequitable interest rate structure, a structure designed to pamper the private corporate sector, and which is biased against agricultural sector and the small borrowers generally. This paradoxical situation was the result of mindless implementation of Basel norms without adaptation of concepts like 'risks' as understood in the developed world. RBI's *Report on Currency and Finance 2005-06* provides valuable insights into the structure of interest rates. The bulk of bank lending has been taking place, at Sub-BPLR (benchmark prime lending rate). For instance, the share of Sub-BPLR lending increased to 82 per cent by March 2007. While higher credit rated corporates are setting credit at Sub-BPLR rates, agriculture and small industry and other small borrowers are generally charged BPLR, or in some cases, above BPLR rates. To quote from the RBI Report (2006): 'to compensate for such Sub-BPLR lending, other segments are charged higher rates of interest, thus leading to cross subsidisation of the economically well-off borrowers by the economically poor borrowers.' This is indeed disturbing especially when the objective of both the inclusive growth in the real sector as envisaged in the Eleventh Plan and financial inclusion is to promote growth with equity. Although this inequitable situation was mollified to some extent by the Government providing interest rate subvention since 2008-09 to ensure that farmers get short-term crop loan up to Rs. 3 lakh at 7 per cent, the basic issue remains. Interestingly enough, none of the reformers of financial sector has identified the problem. It is to the credit of RBI that they brought out the problem in the open and appointed a Working Group, in April 2008 to look into the issue.

Fiscal Inequity

The Indian fiscal system is distinguished by the fact that dividends received by individuals are totally exempt from income tax without any limit. Similarly, there are exemptions without limit, from long-term capital gains from the stock market. Thus, persons receiving thousands of crores of rupees of dividend income are totally free from income tax, while those earning modest incomes from professions are taxed at high rates. These exemptions are sought to be justified on the ground that they foster the development of equity market. The ostensible rationale is that since corporates have already paid the tax, taxing dividend income of individuals would be tantamount to double taxation. This is a specious argument. In the idiom of public finance, corporates and individuals are distinct entities and hence, they ought to be taxed separately. Dr. S.S. Tarapore, former

Deputy Governor of RBI, has correctly argued that unlimited exemptions of dividend income are incongruous with distributive justice and are nothing short of fiscal atrocity.

Import of Gold

One of the most retrogressive reforms introduced during the period is the liberalisation of the import of gold. The annual average level of imports of gold works out to a staggering figure of $5 billion. Import of gold is in a way definancialisation of savings: because financial savings which could have been channelled to productive purposes, would be diverted to unproductive investment in gold. Today, in metropolitan and bigger towns there are more jewellery shops than grocery shops. Surely, the WTO did not prescribe the liberalisation of gold imports. Even public sector banks are encouraged to sell gold coins. Are we exporting food grains to finance the import of gold? This is a clear case of perversion of priorities in economic reforms, or the ugly face of reforms—a face that has nothing to do even remotely with development. Nobody, of course, would advocate a total ban on import of gold but what is required is restraint on the magnitude of imports. Government does not have to go out of the way to encourage the import of gold.

Overall, these reforms like low interest rate regime for the corporate elite, artificial props to develop the capital market and exemption without limit for the dividend income from tax, reflect private corporate sector-centred punditry. Milton Friedman syndrome?

Let us now briefly deal with the India-specific issues both in the financial sector and the real sector.

Revisiting Financial Sector Reforms

What are the implications of the collapse of the American capitalist model, particularly the financial model, for India's reforms? Looking ahead, there is a need for introspection and for a vision on how to move forward: introspection because we have been trying to mimic the American financial model in reforming India's financial sector, particularly in the post-1990s phase. Vision, because in our unabashed attempt to Americanise the Indian financial system our high profile reformers have sadly ignored the nature of the structure of the Indian economy as it has evolved, and India-specific implications for growth. The imperatives of financial inclusion have yet to reassert themselves. Unfortunately, there has been far too much of mimicking American models and copying 'international best practices'. It is high time that we must speak our minds freely about what is right and wrong with the reform path our policymakers have chalked out for us. Otherwise, there is the danger that reforms might crumble under the weight of the egos of the establishment.

When the icons of American and European financial system—commercial banks, investment banks, mortgage houses, and insurance giants—collapsed like a pack of cards, what happened to the mythology built around the private financial institution like capital adequacy norms, Basel norms, provisioning requirements, asset-liability management, risk weighted lending rates, credit rating—all of which we have been trying to superimpose on our banking system? Why did not this paraphernalia of devices emit warning signals that the whole edifice is about to crumble? Prof. Joseph Stiglitz, the Noble Laureate, in a recent interview to an Indian TV Channel said: 'The US financial system collapsed because we did not have a Dr. Reddy at the helm.' The reference here is to Dr. Y.V. Reddy, former Governor of Reserve Bank of India, and there cannot be a better tribute to the management of the Indian financial system. Even those Indian financial wizards who scoffed at Dr. Reddy's 'go slow' policy towards structured financial products have remained to pray.

It is therefore important that we revisit the financial sector reforms and subject the blueprint for reforms to critical scrutiny in the light of these recent developments in the global financial scenario.

The blueprint for reforms has been provided by the Raghuram Rajan Committee which submitted its Report in 2008-09. These high profile reformers, whether it is the Narasimham Committee which submitted its Report in 1998 or the Raghuram Rajan Committee referred to above, share the following four characteristics (Planning Commission, 2008). First, they are soaked in the market theology of the IMF/World Bank: directed credit and credit subsidies should be shunned. Second, they demonstrate a congenital dislike of the public sector in the financial system. Third, their whole focus seems to be on mimicking the financial models of the West, particularly the American model. Fourth, they lack a sense of India's financial history. I have examined the Rajan Committee Report at length and shown that its recommended reforms are unrelated to the India-specific socioeconomic milieu and are inconsistent with the strategy of inclusive growth embodied in the Eleventh Five-Year Plan (2007-2012).[2] The Committee's basic approach to financial sector reforms is flawed. The Report reflects faithfully the market theology of IMF/World Bank, ignoring the India-specific strength of public sector dominated financial system. For instance, 'the majority of this Committee does not see a compelling reason for continuing government ownership' of financial institutions including banks. The Committee has therefore recommended to begin with, selling small public sector banks to the private sector. In the global financial conflagration, when major private sector icons of banks and financial institutions perished both in the US and Europe, the Indian institutions stood, rock-like, unharmed. Indian public sector banks have made us proud. How incongruous such illogical advocacy of privatisation sounds in the light of global financial crisis.

As Governor of RBI (2009) emphasises: 'India's banking system remains healthy, well-capitalised, resilient and profitable. Credit markets have been functioning well and banks have been expanding credit notwithstanding the perceptions in some quarter of lack of adequate credit from banks to the commercial sector.'

It is to the credit of the Indian public sector banks that they have been able to successfully blend the objectives of social banking with the market philosophy of optimising profitability. It is time that our high profile reformers realise that banking efficiency is ownership neutral. Where is then the case for privatisation? There is very little intellectual support for such proposals for privatisation. In fact, the view is gaining ground that banks should be treated as public utilities.

In a similar rein, echoing faithfully the Washington consensus, the Rajan Committee Report recommends that the RBI should abdicate its development responsibilities and concentrate exclusively on control of inflation. This recommendation also has no intellectual support.

---

2. Mujumdar (2008).

Clearly, the Rajan Committee Report should be set aside. Perhaps, it would be useful to set up a new committee headed by 'Dr. Reddy like experts' to provide an alternative blueprint for future financial reforms—reforms which would be in consonance with the inclusive growth strategy in the real sector. While on this subject a reference may be made to Prof. Robert J. Shiller's work which advocates the democratisation of finance or making financial markets 'work for the benefits of the common person.'[3]

Three Core Issues

In the contemporary financial scenario in India, there are three core issues: inclusive growth or broad-based, decentralised growth in the real sector, the new architecture of the financial system to facilitate such growth, and the inequitable interest rate structure. Logically, the reinvention of the next generation financial sector reforms should have emerged from a holistic analysis of these three core issues. Judged by these criteria, high profile reformers have frittered away their energies on a random assortment of recommendations: some relevant, some not so relevant, mainly aimed at mimicking the 'best practices' of banking in the developed world.

In terms of priorities, developing a market for complex structured credit products like credit derivatives, important as it is, can wait; but addressing these core issues cannot brook any delay in terms of food and employment security, and in terms of reducing poverty. Inclusive growth in real sector has now become a growth and development imperative: growth, because a high GDP growth like the 8 or 9 per cent targeted in the Eleventh Plan can be sustained only if other sectors or segments of the economy, which have been sluggish because of a number of reasons, including policy neglect, can be activated and development, because this is perhaps the best route by which bulk of the poor can be provided with livelihood and food security. In other words, we can no longer depend on 'autonomous' forces for growth of the real sector, this growth has to be policy-induced with a view to enabling sections of the population, whom the growth process has bypassed, to fully engage themselves with the development process. The trickle-down theory or percolation theory of growth is dead. While wealth

3. Maurio (2008).

may accumulate, men may decay. An interventionist and proactive policy is therefore warranted. This should be the starting point for designing what are now called the next generation financial sector reforms. In this context, the contemporary experience of China is illuminating. China's township and village enterprises (TVEs) provided increasing job opportunities outside agriculture and this phenomenal expansion of non-farm sector played a critical role in reducing poverty.

The unorganised sector holds the key to broad-based decentralised growth. The recent report on the sector spells out that microenterprises—with an investment of below Rs. 0.5 million—constitute 94 per cent of small enterprises in the country and provide employment to 70 million people and contribute 30 per cent of industrial production. Some 40 per cent of exports are contributed by this sector. Despite occupying this central position, these enterprises receive only 2 per cent of net bank credit (GoI, 2007). If additional credit is injected into this sector it may lead not only to higher production, but it may also promote upgradation of technology, improvement in marketing efficiency, and so on.

The micro, small and medium enterprise (MSME) sector has been affected adversely by the recent global financial crisis. MSMEs particularly related to exports like textiles and garments, gems and jewellery, have been facing problems like slackness in demand for their products and delayed payments of dues by large undertakings.

To ensure that the special problems faced by this sector are addressed, there is merit in the proposal to set up a dedicated development finance institution (DFI) with a mandate to provide refinance to banks for on-lending to microenterprises. Such an umbrella institution should be also able, in addition to facilitating adequate flow of credit, to provide consultancy services.

This sector needs specialised treatment because of another reason: it is an amorphous sector with at least three different segments each of which has its own problems. First, there is a wide range of informal enterprises like tailoring shops, tea shops, auto repair centres and flour mills. Second, enterprises in the growth sectors like housing, auto, white goods, pharmaceuticals, etc. The third segment relates to exporting MSME units that have thrived on the global consumption boom. Many of these have been adversely affected by the present global crisis, as mentioned earlier. To cater to these segments, the establishment of a dedicated development finance institution seems appropriate. This may facilitate extending the reach of lending institutions to this sector and also technological upgradation.

The second core issue is the institutional infrastructure. Microfinance is expected to play an important role in promoting financial inclusion and inclusive growth. It is a sort of supplementary credit delivery system that is cost-effective and user-friendly for both banks and the poor borrowers, RBI's initiatives in promoting this channel of credit delivery have centred around two models, namely SHG-Bank Linkage programme and microfinance institutions (MFI) model. At the same time, the corporative credit structure is being reorganised, on the lines recommended by the Vaidyanathan Committee. Similarly, the more recent developments reveal that regional rural banks (RRBs) could become the main institutional mechanism for providing credit to the poor. As Dr. Thingalaya (2007), a professional banker who has made in-depth study of RRBs, puts it: 'The process of their merger at the state level, reducing the number from 196 to 96 has expanded their operational base considerably. The best among them like the Karnataka Vikas Grameen Bank or Pragathi Grameen Bank are comparable to the best grameen bank, anywhere in the world, including the much publicised banks of Bangladesh... out of the 1.29 crore of borrowing accounts handled by them, 1.07 crore or 83 per cent are in the advances group of less than Rs. 25,000.'

The blueprint for the future institutional structure should clearly indicate how the pyramid comprising banks, RRBs, cooperatives, MFIs and SHGs needs to be built. Here again, there are regional variations. SHGs are more prominent in southern states like Andhra Pradesh, while cooperatives are strong in states like Maharashtra. NGOs working in the relevant area may also be linked to the pyramid.

The final point is related to interest rates. At present, there is intense lobbying by the private corporate sector for further reduction in lending rates by banks. It is necessary to caution that this may prove counter-productive. If India's growth story continues to be intact, despite the global financial mess, it is because India has emerged as a high saving economy with gross domestic savings of 34 per cent of GDP. As the recent Growth Commission puts it: 'Capital inflows over the past several decades have a mixed record. Our view is that foreign saving is an imperfect substitute for domestic saving, including public saving to finance the investment a booming economy requires'. In India, investment as a percentage of GDP increased from 25 per cent in 2002-03 to 38 per cent in 2007-08. Of this 13 percentage points increase, as much as 10 percentage points was financed domestically through higher household, public sector and corporate savings. As a result of reducing lending rates, recently, banks have already reduced deposit rates. If banks are compelled to reduce lending rates further, banks may reduce deposit rates even further. Such very low deposit rates and rates on savings accounts may eventually result in shrinking overall savings. This is particularly so because household sector is a major contributor to overall savings and household savings are sensitive to interest rates. We must guard ourselves against this danger.

To sum up, any blueprint for future financial sector reforms cannot be meaningful, if it does not address these three core issues.

Pyramid of Rural Lending Institutions

How should the financial system, particularly commercial banks, respond to the challenge of facilitating inclusive, or, broad-based and decentralised growth in the real sector? The answer to this question can be given in two parts: first, the coverage of households and second, the loan portfolios of banks.

Is universal coverage or 100 per cent of coverage of households by banks, as the RBI seems to interpret it, the answer? I, for one, would demur. Banking sector resources are, and would continue to be, limited. Optimum utilisation of banking sector resources demands a selective approach to credit extension. Ideally, credit should chase productive activities and universal coverage would be tantamount to dehyphenating credit and productive activities: this would not augur well for facilitating inclusive growth. Of course, it is conceded that at present almost 40 per cent of the adult population of the country comprising mainly those with low incomes and those without collateral are unable to access mainstream financial products. Hence, capturing this section should be our long-term objective. In the meanwhile, if credit is made to chase productive activities, we would promote optimal use of banking sector resources. Spreading available resources too thinly, which universal coverage necessarily implies, may defeat this objective. Furthermore, opening 'no-frills' accounts with low charges may be reduced to mere tokenism. In fact, this may add to transaction costs which may provoke banks to raise their general lending rates. The whole approach to universal coverage of households appears flawed. As we have emphasised, we must think in terms of a pyramid of rural lending institutions and financial institutions as a cooperative enterprise by all the institutions involved. Bank's resources may be enabled to reach the rural borrowers, either directly or indirectly, through the use of multiple channels such as SHGs, MFIs, NGOs, farmers' clubs, *panchayats*, etc., as business facilitators or as correspondents.

Second, we need to prioritise sectors or segments of the rural economy which need credit support. Let me illustrate. Foremost among sluggish sectors is agriculture which is central to India's economic development. Future agricultural growth will have to be necessarily water-centric. Five interconnected programmes assume significance in this context: watershed development both macro and micro, rainwater harvesting and conservation, renovation of traditional water bodies, improving water efficiency in public irrigation works, notably in canals, and promotion of micro-irrigation technology like drip and sprinkler irrigation systems.

There is another heterogeneous bunch of projects related to rural development: animal husbandry, horticulture, fisheries, development of wastelands and forests, soil conservation, drainage and flood control, organic farming with organic seed and compost preparation, food processing, storage, ware housing and marketing.

The moot point in providing a list of illustrative segments is that the loan portfolios of banks and other rural lending institutions must begin to reflect the more diversified credit support to these emerging segments and not merely support crop production, important though the latter will continue to be. This involves the inculcation of a new banking culture, with evolving of appropriate procedures and practices, for project identification, appraisal and monitoring.

The building up of the pyramid of rural lending institutions, including banks with all their multi-channels of credit delivery—should be the central theme of the new discourse on next generation financial sector reforms.

The Real Sector

Rediscovering the Mahatma

The ambitious Bharat Nirman programme launched in 2005 marks a radical departure from the Milton Friedman phase. Involving a massive investment of Rs. 1.74 lakh crore, this is a time-bound programme of rural infrastructure development focussing on six subjects: roads, drinking water, irrigation, housing, electricity and telephones. In a way, this symbolises the beginning of the rediscovery of Mahatma Gandhi's philosophy of rural development. This was subsequently supplemented by other flagship schemes for education and health. Sarva Shiksha Abhiyan for education, mid-day meal scheme providing cooked meals to school children, Integrated Child Development Services (ICD) to promote nutritional supplement to children upto the age of six years. The mid-day meal programme covers some 15 crore children. Furthermore, the National Rural Employment Guarantee Act (NREGA), 2005, is the best thing that could have happened to the poor. This guarantees 100 days of employment in a year to every rural household. In 2008-09, it is estimated that about 4.5 crore rural households benefited from the scheme. The culmination of these efforts is reflected in the National Food Security Act Programme proposed by the President of India in her Address to the Parliament on June 4, 2009. This act seeks to provide a statutory basis for a framework which assures food security for all. Every family below the poverty line in rural as well as urban areas will be entitled, by law to 25 kilograms of rice or wheat per month at Rs. 3 per kilogram. In the Budget Speech of June 6, 2009, the Finance Minister assured that the government will come up with the necessary Act and necessary provision or outlay for the programme will be made. Taken together, these measures go a long way towards meeting the basic needs of the poor—a goal set by the Mahatma.

The Budget Speech sums up the new approach to development: '...the UPA Government has gone for a paradigm shift for making the development process more inclusive. It involves creating entitlements backed by legal guarantee to provide basic amenities and opportunities for livelihood to vulnerable sections. *Aam Admi* is now the focus of all our programmes and schemes'. Are we recapturing the rhythm of our old growth song?

From Predatory to Community-Centred Capitalism

The issue of predatory capitalism has assumed a contemporary relevance with the recent fall from grace of the American capitalist image. The word 'predatory' is defined in simple terms 'as addicted to, or characterised by a tendency to exploit or destroy others for one's own gain'. Revelation of corporate crookedness and accounting scandals have shaken the very foundations of the American capitalist model. The depth of degradation to which unbridled corporate greed can lead to has become all too obvious. The Enron, WorldCom and Xerox and Global Crossing exposures have unveiled the ugly side of western style capitalism under which, in the quest for short-term gain, wrongdoings are overlooked. These developments cannot be dismissed, as some apologists of American capitalism seem to be doing, as isolated incidents. Prof. Lester C. Thurow puts it as: 'The Enron and WorldCom are bot abnormalities in a basically sound system—scandals are endemic to capitalism'. The London Economist summed up the situation: 'Chief executives and accountants have become a despised breed less trusted than politicians and journalists'. Again, take the current financial crisis in the US which started as subprime mortgages they could not afford. With incentives for aggressive loan disbursement, banks poured billions of dollars of loans into poor households often with incomplete documents. The unquestioned faith in the status of triple-A credit rating led to buying of billions of structured bonds which later turned out to be worth nothing, since the market for a number of structured products became non-existent during the period of financial meltdown.[4] Thus, not only mortgage houses, but investment banks, accountants and credit raters were also involved in the melodrama. Have the financial professionals also joined the breed of CEOs mentioned above by the Economist?

4. See the excellent article on the subject by Tapan Babu, *Economic and Political Weekly*, November 8, 2008.

The CEO of one of the biggest banks which was sinking helped himself to a hefty bonus. There was public outrage that some executives of an insurance giant were helping themselves with handsome bonuses from out of the bailout package extended by the US government. The automobile giants Ford, Chrysler and General Motors went in their private jets to seek aid from the Congress! The peanuts-monkey philosophers could do well to ponder over the statement of the Financial Services Authority (FSA) in the UK that overgenerous remuneration practices in the financial industry contributed to the market crisis, since they motivated staff to pursue 'unduly risky practices'. The multimillion dollar bonus culture of investment banks has been blamed for contributing to the risky behaviour, which brought about the near-collapse of the world financial system.

Contrast this with the important revolutions that India witnessed since Independence: the Green Revolution of Dr. M.S. Swaminathan, the White Revolution of Dr. Verghese Kurien, the Telecom Revolution of Sam Pitroda, the Satellite Revolution of Prof. Yash Pal and the IT Revolution of Narayana Murthy. None of these were paid princely salaries nor were they motivated by the million rupee bonuses. In fact, Prof. Diwan belongs to this genre of visionaries.

Fortunately, such predatory capitalism is now dead and today's prophets of private sector philosophy disagree with Friedman.

Mahatma Gandhi had distilled the core of Indian philosophy from our ancient scriptures and evolved his own philosophy. In addition to basic needs of the common man being the first charge on the society's resources, he had another important ingredient: the concept of trusteeship. We should hold our wealth as trustees and not as exclusive owners, so that this wealth is available for sharing by others who need it the most. Dr. Swaminathan would also like to add intellectual property rights (IPRs) as well to the concept of wealth.

From times immemorial, Indian philosophy has maintained that the all-round development of a society is best achieved through betterment of the individuals which no doubt includes economic well-being but extends well beyond it. Social conscience must be inculcated among individuals through education at all stages and also professional training. All individuals must be sensitised, at their young age itself, to abject poverty, the squalor, disease, ignorance and illiteracy that surround us. They must begin to think in terms of what is our *dharma* or duty towards alleviating some of the infirmities that affect our less fortunate fellow human beings. Some Asian countries, recently, have introduced in school textbooks lessons on corruption. But that is a narrow and negative concept. We must aim at building a holistic concept of the right conduct.

One of the ancient scriptures of India, the *Brihadaranyaka Upanishad* enjoins us that our life must be guided by the following three *'Da's—Damyata'*, that is control yourself, *'Datta'*, that is give to others, and *'Dayadhvam'*, that is be compassionate. Thus, we must practice self-control, charity and compassion. Collectively, these three characteristics constitute development conscience (Mujumdar, 2004b). Building up such conscience among all sections of the population would go a long way towards evolving a compassionate society—an ideal which the Mahatma sought to achieve.

Incidentally, it is interesting to add here one point that modern social analysts have been confirming, year after year, Denmark's status as a 'happiness superpower' (Welner, 2009). The secret of this achievement is low expectations of Danes who are not trapped in the hedonic treadmill. This modern research merely endorses what traditional Indian philosophy has been advocating centuries ago. It was left to Mahatma Gandhi to distil this wisdom and evolve a practical programme of a code of conduct.

Reordering of Priorities

The current chorus of the powerful lobby seems to be that freed from the Marxist's shackles, the new UPA government should rush in to implement liberalisation reforms. What does this articulate lobby mean by reforms? Disinvestment, privatisation of public sector banks (PSBs); a bigger role for foreign direct investment (FDI) in retail, insurance, aviation and banking; dilution of government equity in profitably run state entities; making Mumbai an international financial centre where multinationals could freely enter; merger of the associate banks of State Bank of India (SBI) with the parent bank so that this bank could compete internationally, based on the principle 'too big to fail', and so on. Are the ghosts of Milton Friedman still haunting our reformers and articulate lobbies?

In the post-collapse phase of the American capitalist model at least, we should be convinced that there is no intellectual support for privatisation *per se*. Diluting public ownership of undertaking is, of course, quite another matter. In this context, it is appropriate to quote the following paragraphs from President's Address to Parliament on June 4, 2009:

'Our fellow citizens have every right to own part of the shares of public sector companies while the government retains majority share holding and control. My Government will develop a roadmap for listing and people-ownership of public sector undertaking, while ensuring that government equity does not fall below 51 per cent. People-ownership is the key word'.

Interpreted in terms of the Mahatma's broad principles, the new Government should shed the inherited ideological baggage and address the more mundane India-specific issues both in the financial and real sectors. I have already outlined the financial sector priorities and let me end by briefly indicating the kind of real sector reforms needed on a priority basis. There are three issues in the broader area of food and water security: watershed development, rural employment and food grains management.

First, even today about 60 per cent of the total cultivated area is rainfed and hence, future agriculture growth will have to be necessarily water-centric. Watershed development is the mother of all water management modes and today it is seen as the principal strategy for holistic development of rainfed areas. Even though we have been making a lot of noise about the programme, in terms of dimensions involved, the progress is tardy. We should therefore, promote a massive programme aimed at covering say, 50 per cent of the total eligible area in the next two years. We could designate the two years 2009-10 and 2010-11 as Watershed Development Years.

Second, National Rural Employment Guarantee Act (NREGA), 2005 is the best thing that could have happened to the rural poor. Happily, the Budget for 2009-10 envisages the expansion of the scheme. Rural connectivity, water harvesting structures, drought proofing, minor and micro-irrigation works are among the activities undertaken under the scheme. Perhaps, it would be good to mandate this scheme to concentrate on watershed development activities in the next two years in the rainfed areas.

Taken together, these would go a long way towards providing water and food security to the poor.

Third, there should be no exports of food grains, except some small quantities of high value commodities like *basmati* rice. Domestic consumption should have the first claim on our production of food grains. Before the threat of bad monsoon during the current year, there was some talk of export of 2 million tonnes of wheat. Hence, this position needs to be reiterated. Furthermore, the Food Corporation of India (FCI) needs to play a proactive role in the management of food grains prices. We seem to treat FCI as a glorified godown keeper. Instead, it should emerge as a market. For instance, with its present huge stocks of rice and wheat of around 50 million tonnes, it should ensure that food grains prices in the open market do not rise to high levels. It should be able to identify pockets of high price rises and by unloading appropriate quantities of food grains in those pockets, it should seek to bring down prices. Thus, it should be able to contain food grain prices within a reasonable band. Finally, forward trading in food grains should be banned. Farmers' decisions regarding crop planning and investment are guided by minimum support prices (MSP) rather than by forward prices (Mujumdar, 2009).

Summing Up

It is an irony of economic history that India which was a pioneer in emphasising 'growth with equity' in its approach to development, much before mainstream development economists caught up with it, should have relapsed into a phase of mindless pursuit of market theology. The period of economic reforms from 1991 to 2004 was the most retrogressive phase, a phase which I have called the Milton Friedman phase. Although India graduated to a high growth league during this phase, it had to pay a heavy price. While wealth accumulated, men decayed. The number of underfed and undernourished people in India rose from 206 million to 230 million during this period. The growth culture itself became toxic. A huge quantity of food grains was exported, at a time when the number of underfed persons increased. Policymakers of the time condemned subsidies for domestic consumption of food grains: but they have no qualms about subsiding export of food grains. The interest rate regime which emerged as a result of reforms pampered the corporate elite and discriminated against the small borrowers, generally. There was fiscal inequity again designed to pamper the dividend earning elite.

The launching of the Bharat Nirman programme in 2005 marked a radical departure from the Milton Friedman phase. Our policymakers, it appears, began to rediscover Mahatma Gandhi. There was the mid-day meal programme for school children, nutritional supplement to children up to the age of six years, and so on. The National Rural Employment Guarantee Act, 2005 was the best that could have happened to the rural poor. The culmination of this journey towards holistic development is the proposed National Food Security Act. I have called this phase the Mahatma Gandhi phase.

There is no generic formula for growth. 'Each country has specific characteristics and historical experiences that must be reflected in its growth strategy.' That is where the philosophy of Mahatma Gandhi for evolving a compassionate society with a value system which resonates to these society's larger concerns acquires contemporary relevance. The collapse of the American capitalist model in 2008 now warrants that we move away from predatory capitalism to what can be broadly described as community-centred capitalism. Let us not be trapped into hedonic treadmill. Our contemporary policymakers should realise that economic efficiency is ownership neutral. There is no intellectual support for privatisation *per se*.

Viewed against this broader background, our agenda for reform would warrant a reordering of priorities both in the real and financial sectors.

The journey towards holistic development takes us well beyond growth models. Evolving a compassionate society, for which the Mahatma struggled, involves betterment of individuals whose life must be guided by the three 'Da's'—*Dasdamyata*, *Datta* and *Dayadhvam*—practice self-control, charity and compassion.

References

FAO (2008). *The State of Food Security in the World*. Rome.

Government of India (2007). *Report on Conditions of Work and Promotion of Livelihood in the Unorganised Sector*. p. 211.

Maurio, Paolo (2008). "From Visionary to Innovator", *Finance and Development*. Washington, D.C.: IMF. December.

Mujumdar, N.A. (2009). "Commodity Futures Market: Dehyphenating Financial Flows and Supply-Demand Fundamentals", in Madhoo Pavaskar (ed.), *Future Markets*. Mumbai.

———. (2008)."Next Generation Financial Sector Reforms and Inclusive Growth", in S. Subrahmanya and B.S. Bhandary (eds.) *Essays in Honour of Prof. S.L.N. Simha*. Bangalore: Southern Economist.

———. (2007). "Inclusive Growth-Development Perspectives in Indian Economy", *Economic Developments in India*. New Delhi: Academic Foundation.

———. (2004a) "Economic Reforms *sans* Development", *Economic Developments in India*. New Delhi: Academic Foundation.

———. (2004b). "The Development Conscience Factor", *Economic Reforms sans Development*. New Delhi: Academic Foundation.

Mujumdar, N.A. and Uma Kapila (eds.) (2007). *Indian Agriculture in the New Millennium*. New Delhi: Academic Foundation.

Planning Commission (2008). *Draft Report of the Committee on Financial Sector Reforms (CFRS)*.

RBI (2009). *Third Quarter Reviw of Monetary Policy* 2008-09. January. p. 20.

———. (2006). *Report on Currency and Finance, 2005-06*. Mumbai: Reserve Bank of India. p. 159.

Sharma, Anand (ed.) (2007). *Gandhian Way: Peace, Non-violence and Empowerment*. New Delhi: Academic Foundation.

Thingalaya, N.K. (2007). "Annuals of a Central Bank", *Indian Economic Journal*, April-June.

Welner, Eric (2009). "Where less means more", *The Times of India*, July 22.

World Bank (2008). *The Growth Report: Strategies Growth and Inclusive Development*. Washington, D.C. p. 2.

Seventh Prof. G.S. Diwan Memorial Lecture, September 12, 2009.

8 Austerity, Affluence and the Mahatma

Currently, there is a renewal of the debate on austerity in public life. What sparked of the debate was this: Finance Minister Pranab Mukherjee asked both S.M. Krishna, Minister for External Affairs and Shashi Tharoor, Minister of State for External Affairs to move out of the luxurious suites of a five star hotel in which they were staying for the last 100 days or so. This was an interim arrangement till official accommodation would be made available to them. Again, ministers and MPs were advised to travel by economy class rather than executive class. This led to Tharoor facetiously stating on a microblogging site that he travelled 'cattle-class in solidarity with the holy cows'. In defence of the ministers, a view has been put forward that since they were meeting the hotel charges out of their personal finances, and not charging the government, why should there be any objection?

These arguments and counter-arguments show that we are treating 'austerity and affluence' as merely phrases in a dialectic process, ignoring their larger philosophic import. It was Mahatma Gandhi who provided, by both precept and practice, a strong case for austerity in our blessed land of poverty and hunger. Recent FAO estimates show that the number of underfed and undernourished people in India has risen from 260 million in 1990-1992 to 230.5 million in 2003-2005, an increase of 24 million. Hunger and poverty are an affront to civilised society. Moreover, the period 1990-91 to 2003-04 is a period of economic reforms and liberalisation of the economy and our reformers proclaim that India has graduated to a high-growth economy. Thus, it is not merely the drought of the current year but the self-contradiction of affluence and poverty which warrants a regime of austerity, not merely as a temporary measure but as a medium-term measure till poverty is eliminated. We must rediscover Mahatma Gandhi and learn to look beyond drought-related austerity—as some apologists of the current austerity measures seem to be suggesting—to evolving a society with a value system which resonates to these larger concerns of the community as a whole. I have spelt out these issues in my Diwan Memorial Lecture (September 12, 2009) (chapter 7). In this chapter, I seek to outline the contours of the main discourse.

Mahatma and Economic Reforms

Mahatma's approach to poverty alleviation provides the starting point of the imperatives of austerity.

Bhikhu Parekh has admirably encapsulated the poverty profile, as sketched by the Mahatma (see chapter 3: 32).

Alleviation of poverty or elimination of hunger thus becomes a collective responsibility of the community—not merely of the government. Concern for the community as a whole is the foundation of a compassionate society.

The period of economic reforms, 1990-91 to say 2004 which witnessed mindless pursuit of unbridled market theology by our policymakers was the most retrogressive phase in Indian economic history. That is when the magnitude of the underfed and undernourished population increased sizeably.

During the first phase of reforms in India between 1991-2006, our policymakers were soaked in the market theology. The focus was on liberalisation, market-led growth, fiscal correction, promotion of private and foreign investment, development of capital market and generally, creation of an environment of consumerism. More basic issues of development were overlooked, which led to neglect of agriculture, deceleration of public investment in agriculture and in the flow of credit to agriculture, disdain for subsidies, whether food subsidy or credit subsidy, focussing on jobless growth, and disregard for the elementary principles of food security.

This period also witnessed perversion of priorities. The most disturbing policy was the export of a huge quantity of 29 million tonnes of food grains during the three years 2001-02 to 2003-04. This was at a time when the number of underfed was increasing. As a matter of fiscal prudence, the policymakers cut down subsidies for domestic consumption of food grains. The same policymakers had no qualms about subsidising export of food grains! The interest rate regime was inequitable, designed to pamper the corporate elite and biased against small borrowers generally. For instance, a small farmer was made to pay a 12 per cent interest rate, at a time when a triple-A rated company raised money from banks at 6 per cent.

Rediscovering the Mahatma

Fortunately, the retrogressive phase 1991-2004 came to an end in 2005 when our policymakers began to rediscover the Mahatma.

The ambitious Bharat Nirman programme launched in 2005 marks a radical departure from the earlier phase. In a way, this symbolises the beginning of the rediscovery of Mahatma Gandhi's philosophy of rural development. This was subsequently supplemented by other flagship schemes for education and health. Sarva Shiksha Abhiyan for education, Mid-day Meal scheme providing cooked meals to school children, Integrated Child Development Services (ICDs) to promote nutritional supplement to children upto the age of six years. The Mid-day Meal programme covers some 15 crore children. Furthermore, the National Employment Guarantee Act (NREGA), 2005 is the best thing that could have happened to the poor. This guarantees 100 days of employment in a year to every rural household. In 2008-09, it is estimated that about 4.5 crore rural households benefited from the scheme. The culmination of these efforts is reflected in the National Food Security Act proposed by the President of India in her Address to the Parliament on June 4, 2009. This Act seeks to provide a statutory basis for a framework which assures food security for all. Every family below the poverty line in rural as well as urban areas will be entitled, by law to 25 kilograms of rice or wheat per month at Rs. 3 per kilogram. In the Budget Speech of June 6, 2009, the Finance Minister assured that the government will come up with the necessary Act and necessary provision or outlay for the programme will be made. Taken together, these measures go a long way towards meeting the basic needs of the poor—a goal set by the Mahatma.

Beyond the Growth Models

Are we recapturing the rhythm of our old growth and development songs, the tune for which was set by Mahatma Gandhi nearly 100 years ago? The point is that in our approach to development, we have to go beyond econometric growth models.

Mahatma Gandhi had distilled the core of Indian philosophy from our ancient scriptures and evolved his own philosophy. In addition to basic needs of the common man being the first charge on the society's resources, he had another important ingredient: the concept of trusteeship. We should hold our wealth as trustees and not as exclusive owners, so that this wealth is available for sharing by others who need it the most.

Reordering Priorities

This is a defining moment in the history of global economic system. The collapse of the capitalist model of the American economy in 2008 is disturbing enough for us to introspect whether our mindless pursuit of market theology was justified at all. That is where the contemporary relevance of the Gandhian model of development becomes apparent. We must move away from predatory capitalism to a community-centred capitalism, to community-centred development. This involves reordering of the development priorities. As illustrative of such reordering, three issues in the broader area of food and water security may be briefly mentioned: watershed development, rural employment and food grains management. The current year's drought has exposed our vulnerability to monsoon. Watershed development is the mother of all water management modes. We should promote a massive programme aimed at covering say, 50 per cent of the total eligible area in the next two years. National Rural Employment Scheme is the best thing that could have happened to the rural poor. It would be good to mandate this scheme to focus on watershed development activities in the rainfed areas. Finally, in terms of food grains management, there should be no export of food grains, except some small quantities of high value commodities like *basmati* rice. The Food Corporation of India (FCI) should grow up from being a glorified godown keeper to emerge as a market maker in the area of food grains prices. It should ensure that food grains prices in the open market would move in a narrow band. Taken together, these three measures would go a long way towards ensuring water and food security to the poor.

9 Disinvestment: A Second Look

Let us begin with the question 'Is Privatisation or Disinvestment the Answer to the Ills of the Indian Economy?'. Today, if we look at the media and the pronouncements of some policymakers, they are building up a mythology about privatisation, a mythology about disinvestment, that as if disinvestment is a cure to the ills of the Indian economy. For example, they say 'Don't delay the privatisation of the petroleum companies, because that will give a wrong signal to foreign investment'. Foreign investors may be turned away because we are not going ahead with the petroleum companies' disinvestment. Disinvestment, they say, is going to give a stimulus to the inflow of foreign investment. Second, if we bring in a number of public sector units (PSUs) into the private sector, the capital market would boom, because not only the availability of shares in the capital market will increase, but also the kind of expectations of the investors or the buoyant market expectations. So these kind of incentives to inflow of foreign investment and expectations of a boom in the capital market are built around this so-called disinvestment theory. Similarly, the other—perhaps one of the most flimsiest argument that is being made in favour of disinvestment is that today, the fiscal deficit of the Centre is going to touch almost 6 per cent of the GDP as against the budgeted level of 4.5 per cent. If we generate some money by selling these PSUs, those resources could be used to bridge the gap in the fiscal deficit. This is a most unfortunate argument because in fact, we should not sell our family silver to buy groceries. In other words, if we are going to sell these PSUs only to breach the budget deficit, it is the most unproductive way of using our resources. We should only use resources generated by the sale of PSUs for either fresh investment or to clear long-term debt of the government. In fact, as the Reserve Bank of India (RBI) proposed earlier, if we are going to disinvest on a big scale, we should create a separate sinking fund into which all these resources would go and these resources will be utilised to clear or bring down long-term government debt or to make fresh investments. We cannot use these resources for supporting government consumption. The point therefore is, that these myths being built around disinvestment, is giving a sort of a wrong impression; we are giving an unnecessarily exaggerated importance to the whole philosophy of privatisation. As students of economics or teachers in commerce and business schools or even business management professionals, we should try to give a proper perspective to the whole question of privatisation or disinvestment. In other words, in the macroeconomic management of the economy, what precise role privatisation should play and what kind of an approach should we develop towards disinvestment in the future development policy?

Today, the whole impression seems to be that private sector as such is the paragon of virtue and public sector is the repository of inefficiency. This is certainly not true because even in America, the land of capitalism, the image of the private corporate sector has suddenly taken a beating, with the exposures of Enron, Xerox Corporation, WorldCom and so on. The revelations have shown the depths of degradation to which, unbridled corporate greed can lead. We are trying to emulate that system. Today, even business economists of America are worried about the behaviour of American Corporation. According to Prof. Lester C. Thurow of the Sloan School of Management, MIT, 'The Enron and WorldComs are not abnormalities in a basically sound system. Scandals are endemic to capitalism.' In other words, let us not be under the impression that the private sector is the paragon of virtue and therefore, any change from the public sector to the private sector is a welcome change. We should disabuse our minds of this idea. Particularly in terms of the American models, the worst part of it was the nexus between the corporate entity, the accounting firm and the capital market. Especially one of the world's fifth largest accounting firm Arthur Anderson's collapse has brought out the fact that if any particular company wants to mislead the investors, it can do so with the help of a complying accounting firm. That is how the whole capital market in America boomed, because of accounting frauds and the investors were taken for a ride. Even in a country where investors are supposed to be very vigilant, and the media supposed to keep the investors well informed, this kind of nexus between the corporate entity, the accounting firm and the capital market has really shattered the very image of the corporate sector. As here we are trying to imitate the American capitalist model, we are really committing a blunder, if we go under this kind of impression. In India, of course, we have our own counterparts of Enron or WorldCom, though on a small scale. Certainly the private sector as such cannot be regarded as the abode of all virtues and the public sector the abode of vices. We, as students of the subject, should lend this perspective to the whole question of privatisation. The basic lesson that we have to learn from the recent happenings in the American corporate world is: any doctrinaire approach to privatisation, as we seem to be adopting now, is as unjustifiable as the doctrinaire approach to public sector enterprises we had adopted earlier. We should recall that our slogan was that the commanding heights of the economy should be in the public sector. That thesis is history now. That kind of doctrine has proved to be a false start. But let us not go to the other extreme and say that let us give up all economic activities of the government and only concentrate on law and order or justice. So what should we do? What should be our guiding principles? At this point, we should look at one or two serious criticisms that are being made of the Nehruvian philosophy of which the commanding heights of the economy was a core principle. Because historically, some of the substantial achievements we have made would not have been possible, if the government had not stepped into these businesses. For example, take power or irrigation and infrastructure, like roads, railways and so on. At that point of time when we began planning in 1951, no private sector was in a position to undertake any of these activities and historically therefore, there was sufficient justification for the government to get into these activities. But we must recognise this historical role and stop blaming today that the whole Nehruvian approach of bringing in commanding heights of economy into the public sector was wrong. If today things have deteriorated, we should probe into what exactly has gone wrong and then try to correct those mistakes in the management of public sector. The other reason of the limitation of managerial ability on the part of government also is a myth, according to me. There is no shortage of entrepreneurs available to the government; for example, today it is of no use saying that we can get business management experts only by paying one lakh per month. This is again a concept we have borrowed from the American folklore. Because even small firms in India have done well. How has the software sector in India developed without any assistance of the government and without any assistance of the financial sector? Even commercial banks refused to finance software companies in the beginning. Despite these handicaps, the software sector bloomed into a major source of foreign exchange earning and employment, software experts themselves evolved into management experts and so on. They are internationally competitive. So there is no shortage of entrepreneurial talent in the country. Fortunately, we have a number of highly educated, qualified people. Given the right environment, such people could flourish. The point is that once we provide the right sort of environment for this talent to flourish and flower, we will be able to get the right sort of people from the management pool or economists. So we should not think that managerial ability would be a constraint on public sector enterprises, provided again we adopt the right sort of approach in choosing persons. So if we look at from this point of view—what kind of an approach we could adopt towards privatisation or disinvestments—the basic approach should be that if there is a chronically loss-making PSUs by all means let us sell it off. Then the other thing is, if there are some PSUs, which are sick or are loss-making, let us go into the reasons behind the sickness. We have success stories of BHEL and HMT. If they could do such an excellent job in their respective fields, what is lacking today? We will find that some bureaucratic or political meddling in the management of PSUs is really a major stumbling block in efficient or profitable management of these concerns. For example, Indian bankers are second to none in the world, in terms of professional competence. Then why are our public sector banks today making losses? Why are they not maintaining the image of efficient functioning? These are some of the issues. Therefore, reform of the PSUs in terms of management, resources and hierarchy that we have built into the structure of these units is mandatory. This element of reform of PSUs should be also one of the important ingredients of our approach to privatisation. If PSUs could be cured of political or bureaucratic meddling, and given autonomy in terms of their own day-to-day management, there is no reason why they could not function as efficiently as the private sector units and perhaps may prove much better. That is one of the important things, which nobody talks about today while discussing privatisation.

Third, there are some classic cases, e.g., take the famous case of the Industrial Development Bank of India (IDBI). At one time, the image of the

IDBI was so good that even some foreign countries sent their own experts to study the functioning of IDBI with a view to replicating it in their own countries. Even Singapore had sent its experts to study IDBI. Today it is almost a sick unit. Why did it happen? Not because it is in the public sector, but because we have mismanaged it. There is a lot of political and bureaucratic interference in the functioning of IDBI and there is no autonomy to the board of the IDBI. Thus, there are some wrong policies pursued in the name of reforms like in 1992, withdrawal of RBI assistance to IDBI. The quality of management of the PSUs have to be looked into to be able to come out with some reforms. Let us not dismiss them as unprofitable, or/and inefficient. Whether these could be turned into profitable units by modification of policies, that is the kind of criteria that we need to apply. Lastly, in terms of serving the interests of all the stakeholders in the economy, I think PSUs do much better than private sector units, because when we talk about private sector, we go by the profitability criteria. But profitability alone is not the end objective of all development efforts that we are making. We not only have to protect investors and management, but look at it in terms of welfare of the society as a whole. How do these particular units, the corporate units perform? That should be also one of the important criteria for judging the efficiency of these both sectors. Because as we know that today, the philosophy of serving all stakeholders has become one of the essential profiles of a good corporate unit whether it is in public or private sector. So looking at the welfare of all stakeholders in the unit or in the economy, the functioning of a particular unit should also be one of the important considerations, by which, one could judge the efficiency of a particular unit. In other words, we should try to look at privatisation as only a small segment in the macroeconomic management of the economy, not as the main thrust of our development policy, as the current policymakers or as the media is emphasising today. For example, to give one very obvious example, we have today more than 60 million tonnes of food grains with the public sector, i.e., the Food Corporation of India (FCI). In a country where millions of people are underfed and undernourished, such a mountain of surplus food grains is an anachronism. But today in the media we do not see any discussion on how exactly could we productively use these food grains. Even our current policymakers choose to maintain a studied silence on the issue. Stocks of food grains could be utilised, atleast partly, to alleviate the hunger problem. Providing food to the needy remains a major issue, in terms of economic problems. But the media is more obsessed with privatisation than this more fundamental issue. Let us not be guided by the media. Because it is also influenced by lobby or lobbies. There is a distinct lobby, which is interested in getting some of these PSUs, into the private sector orbit and therefore, this kind of propaganda or publicity is built up around the issue. Let us not be led by this mythology, which is being built around the privatisation philosophy. Let us look at it as students of economics and management professionals and adopt a rational approach as to how exactly we could proceed with privatisation, and that is why I call this whole approach as a 'systemic' approach to privatisation and not privatisation, which is led by a 'doctrinaire' approach.

This is the Inaugural Address at the Seminar on "Disinvestment: A Second Look" organised by Lala Lajpat Rai Institute of Management, Mumbai, 24th February 2003.

Part II

Financial Sector Reforms

10 Financial Inclusion

A Systemic Perspective

Introduction

It appears that idioms and metaphors of development economics keep on changing from time to time. Suddenly, the phrase 'inclusive growth' has become fashionable as is reflected in the title of the Draft Approach Paper to the Eleventh Five-Year Plan (2007-2012)—'Towards Faster and More Inclusive Growth'. This is perhaps a new label to the rather old-fashioned concept of 'broad-based and decentralised growth' which some of us have been advocating for many years (Mujumdar, 2004: 109). Financial inclusion can be regarded as a counterpart of the inclusive growth in the real sector. The current official discourses on financial inclusion seem to suggest that financial inclusion involves drawing up a 'plan for designing and delivering credit to every household that seeks credit from lending institutions' (GoI, 2006). I would seek to argue that such an approach obfuscates the very rationale underlying the need for inclusive growth in the real sector. Analytically, we should clearly distinguish financial inclusion from such concepts as 'food security' which aims at providing access to food to everybody in the country. Financial inclusion does not certainly mean 'credit security'. Our financial resources are not only limited but will also continue to be limited. Credit deployment among different segments should therefore be guided by the principle of optimal utilisation of credit. Extending the reach of the banking system would therefore necessarily involve a process of selection, prioritisation and according preferential treatment to certain sectors or segments of the economy. The first step in this direction perhaps, is to identify the sectors or segments of the economy which have not received adequate attention so far, because of a variety of factors including policy neglect, but which deserve to be focussed on in the new strategy of inclusive growth. All those involved in the development of the Indian economy—banks, cooperative credit institutions, development finance institutions, NGOs, Panchayati Raj Institutions (PRIs) and development administrators will have to rethink their own strategies to reach these sectors or segments. Financial inclusion becomes meaningful only if the development of credit is guided by such a systemic perspective. Again, such thrust on neglected sectors or segments of the economy cannot be allowed to proceed in a slow, gradual, incremental manner: but there should be a big bang. There is a sense of urgency in enabling the sections of population, whom the growth process has bypassed, to fully engage themselves with the development process. I will try to outline the contours of such a systemic perspective.

Inclusive growth in the real sector is a welcome corrective to the 'growth-only' policies of the last 15 years since the introduction of economic reforms in 1991. This phase when the policy focus was on liberalisation, market-led growth, fiscal correction promotion of private and foreign investment, development of the capital market and creation of an environment of consumerism, can be categorised as an 'era of exclusion'. For instance, during this phase, a large number of small farmers were pushed out of commercial banks' loan-portfolio (Mujumdar, 2001). Further more, a large number of poor families were thrown out of the public distribution system (PDS) because of the new definition of 'below the poverty line' (BPL) families. Due to the continuous raising of the issue prices of food grains, the concessionally priced food grains became increasingly inaccessible to the poor (Sen, 2002). Ironically enough, India, which is the abode of the largest number of chronically underfed and undernourished persons in the world, exported a huge quantity of 27 million tonnes of food grains during the three consecutive years 2001-02 to 2003-04. Inspired by market theology, Indian policymakers appear to have become cortically blind during this phase in the sense that their eyes could see but their brains could not register the image of what they saw. Alas! little did our policymakers realise that brand of development economics, founded on market theology, which only exhorts us to raise the production of food grains, without ever bothering to find out the *modus operandi* by which food grains so produced could reach the bulk of the needy, is of little relevance to the contemporary Indian economic situation.

It is perhaps the search for an alternative paradigm of growth which has now led the policymakers to opt for 'inclusive growth', which is pro-poor and which may provide an answer to the dilemma faced by the market-led development approach.

Chinese Experience

In this context, the contemporary experience of China is illuminating. China, whose macroeconomic parameters were comparable to those of India, provides the most fascinating example of such inclusive growth. Today, China's manufacturing power is reshaping the world economy. The world capital labour ratio has nearly halved because of the incorporation of its new labour force in the global economy (Maxwell, 2006). Analytically, what is important to highlight is that this impressive growth in manufacturing and even the double-digit GDP growth sustained over more than two decades would not have been able, by themselves, to make a significant dent on levels of unemployment or of poverty. It was the vibrant rural non-farm sector which played a critical role in the success story of drastically reducing poverty and unemployment. China's township and village enterprises (TVEs) provided increasing job opportunities outside agriculture thereby augmenting sources of household income. The phenomenal growth of this sector is demonstrated by the fact that its contribution to GDP rose to nearly one-third of total GDP in 2004, from practically zero in 1952 (Braun *et al.*, 2006). As a result of this development rural poverty which was 33 per cent in 1971 declined sharply to only 3 per cent in 2001.

Official Discourse in India

The genesis of the current official discourses on financial inclusion in India can be traced to the Budget Speech of Minister of Finance P. Chidambaram (GoI, 2006).

> The findings of the NSS 59th Round (2003) reveal that out of the total number of cultivator households only 27 per cent receive credit from formal sources and 22 per cent from informal sources. The remaining households, namely small and marginal farmers, have virtually no access to credit. With a view to bringing more cultivator households within the banking fold, I propose to appoint a Committee on Financial Inclusion. The Committee will be asked to identify the reasons for exclusion, and suggest a plan for designing and delivering credit to every household that seeks credit from lending institutions.

The Reserve Bank of India's (RBI) conception of financial inclusion appears to be even more restrictive. As Y.V. Reddy (2006) put it 'The Mid-Term Review of October 2005 had urged all banks to make basic banking facilities accessible to vast sections of population with a view to achieving greater financial inclusion.' But the measures announced by Governor in April 2006 were in the nature of procedural simplification. For instance, banks should provide a basic 'no-frills' account with nil or very low minimum balances as well as charges, a simplified general purpose credit card (GCC) should be provided without insistence on collateral or purpose and so on. RBI hoped that these measures would go some way towards 'achieving greater financial inclusion'.

This obsession of the monetary authorities with credit reaching all rural households is clearly reflected in the more recent advice of RBI (2006a) to the State Level Bankers' Committee (SLBC) conveners in all states/UTs 'to identify at least one district in their area for achieving 100 per cent financial inclusion by providing a 'no-frills' account and a general purpose credit card (GCC)'.

Basket of Segments

The crux of the whole discussion on inclusive growth in the real sector is that even if the 8 per cent GDP growth targeted in the Eleventh Plan is sustained in the coming years, and export growth is maintained at, say, 15 to 20 per cent, the organised sectors like large and medium industries including service sectors like IT sector, etc., can do precious little to tackle problems of unemployment, poverty and hunger. In other words, jobs generated autonomously by the normal growth process will fall far short of the requirement. The policy thrust will perforce have to be on decentralised, broad-based growth, that is, 'inclusive growth', on which the Eleventh Plan is expected to focus. The financial system, including banks would need to gear itself up to cater to the new segments to facilitate such a growth process. The segments may have been neglected so far and hence banks may not be familiar with their credit requirements, methods of processing, and appraisal of projects relating to these segments. Extending credit support to those segments is in essence what constitutes 'financial inclusion'.

The first step in this direction, as mentioned above, is to identify the segments of the rural economy which deserve to be focussed on in the new strategy. This bunch of segments cannot be called non-farm sector in the strict sense; the important distinction is that banks or lending institutions should look forward to financing sectors or segments beyond crop production. Obviously, the package of such segments cannot be identical with that of Chinese because of different resource endowments, and also priorities. As illustrative of the segments on which banks need to focus, we could identify the following.

Even after the potential of large and medium irrigation projects is fully exploited, about 60 per cent of cultivable land would continue to be under the dry farming system. Hence, future agricultural growth will have to be necessarily water-centric. Five interconnected programmes assume significance in this context: (i) watershed development programmes, both micro and macro; these if properly implemented, have the potentiality of providing livelihood security in the rainfed regions; (ii) renovation of all water bodies linked to agriculture, which have presently fallen into disuse; (iii) correcting the deterioration of public irrigation works, notably state canal systems due to cumulative neglect of repair and maintenance. Poor maintenance has led to loss of water through seepage and hence water use efficiency is very low at around 25 to 40 per cent, as against the 65 per cent norm attainable; (iv) rainwater harvesting and conservation; and (v) equally important is the need to raise water use efficiency, by promoting micro-irrigation technology on a large scale through drip and sprinkler irrigation systems (Mujumdar, 2006).

The implications for financial flows are clear. For instance, promotion of micro-irrigation technology deserves priority attention by banks and other financial institutions. About 1.2 million hectares have been covered under micro-irrigation so far. The target is to increase the coverage to 3 million hectares by the end of the Tenth Plan (2002-2007) and to 14 million hectares by the end of the Eleventh Plan. Such a quantum jump in coverage can be facilitated only if banks and other concerned financial institutions extend adequate credit support to the manufacture of sprinkler irrigation equipment and their distribution.

The second set of segments relates to what can be broadly called diversification of agriculture. This is an inclusive concept which would encompass, animal husbandry, horticulture, dairy development, fisheries and development of waste lands and forests, plantations, soil conservation, drainage and flood control, organic farming with organic seed and compost preparation, food processing, storage, warehousing and marketing. All these impinge directly or indirectly on agricultural development and rural incomes in general. These wide range of activities are illustrative of the segments from which the demand for investment credit and working capital may emanate and bankers and other rural lending institutions should prepare themselves for meeting these requirements.

Inclusive Growth and Credit Policy

Before we take up for discussion the challenges that financing of segments of the real sector listed above, throw to the making of credit policy, three aspects of financial inclusion ought to be spelt out. First, we began with the proposition that financial inclusion is a growth and development imperative. Basically, this is so because broad-based and decentralised growth in the real sector is perhaps the only route to sustainability of high growth and development. Growth imperative because sustainability of, say, 8 per cent overall GDP growth is contingent upon growth in the segments we have discussed above which are at present sluggish. Take the case of agriculture. While the Tenth Plan stipulates an average annual growth of 4 per cent, the actual average for the first three years works out to some 2 per cent. Perhaps growth in the irrigated fertile lands like the Punjab, Haryana region has reached a sort of plateau. The thrust for further growth must now come from the rainfed, drylands. It is in this context, that watershed development, rain harvesting, renovation of water bodies, etc., assume significance. Development imperative because this is the one route by which benefits of growth are going to be spread widely. Projects relating to these segments offer higher employment in the rural sector where poverty is concentrated and ensure food security to the poor through enlargement of their purchasing power. Inclusive growth in the real sector thus ensures growth with equity.

The second aspect relates to viability. The illustrative segments we have chosen to discuss would offer projects which would be viable and therefore eminently bankable. For instance, take any project relating to water-centric development of agriculture. The economic returns on these projects would be such as to justify the investment on these projects. In addition, there is the consideration that many of these are in the nature of social overhead capital investment. The projects we have discussed are economically viable and the credit policymakers need not be apologetic about persuading banks or other lending institutions to extend credit support to such projects.

The third aspect relates to the scope of financial inclusion, which has a much wider connotation, than the coverage of all cultivators by institutional credit. The term 'agriculture' should be construed in an extended sense which would, of course, include allied sectors like livestock, fisheries, poultry and forests. Raising rural income levels would involve not only higher agricultural growth but also raising production levels of products like milk, meat, poultry vegetables and fruits. Besides promoting diversification of agriculture, there is the need for value addition for increasing rural employment and incomes. Post-harvest activities such as storage, transportation, processing and marketing become important in this context. In addition, investment avenues which go someway towards raising directly or indirectly the production capabilities of agriculture will have to be covered. As the recent Committee on Capital Formation in Agriculture (GoI, 2003) has pointed out that the emphasis should be on 'capital formation for agriculture' in contrast to our conventional approach of 'capital formation in agriculture'. 'The new strategy for agricultural growth and diversification of agriculture from traditional crop cultivation to horticulture, etc., would require more investment in cold storage, rural road, communication, marketing network and facilities, warehouses, etc. Simultaneously, efforts should be made to revitalise agriculture through introduction of biotechnology and other innovations. This would require substantial increase in investment in research and development for agriculture.'

The loan-portfolios of banks and other rural lending institutions, must begin to reflect the more diversified credit support to these emerging areas and not merely support to crop production, important though it will continue to be.

The task of credit policymakers would be indeed arduous. To begin with, the composition of the basket of segment is so heterogeneous that

RBI cannot think in terms of targets for segments or sub-segments. RBI will have to perhaps evolve region-specific baskets and depend upon its persuasive proclivities to induce banks to finance such projects. The focus of policy in the coming years would have to be: first, on sensitising banks about the emerging segments of the economy which need credit support; second, to persuade them to extend credit support to these segments. The task of RBI is difficult because the segments are not 'glamourous' like the corporate sector or the export sector. Again, these are segments with which banks are not familiar and hence, initially at least, banks will have to make special efforts to evolve appropriate mechanisms to reach these segments. This brings us to the new architecture of the rural credit delivery system.

Another question which arises in this context is that when microcredit institutions are involved in the rural credit delivery system, is there a need for instituting some sort in credit guarantee schemes, and/or providing interest rate subsidies? An interesting example is the Chinese experiment of providing microcredit to laid-off workers to enable them to start new businesses. This credit was supported by guarantee scheme and was also subsidised (Xiaoling, 2004). Whether such incentives, could be provided initially to expand microfinance institutions (MFIs) in India needs to be explored.

New Architecture of the Credit Delivery System

The new segments of the economy on which lending institutions including banks, need to focus are scattered and dispersed widely. And commercial banks cannot easily access them. Moreover, underlying the present sickness of the rural credit system are two core causes: high transaction costs of such dispersed lending in small amounts, and poor recovery performance. More recent experience has demonstrated that both these problems can be tackled effectively through the instrumentality of microcredit institutions. The experiment of microfinance through the conduit of self-help groups (SHGs) has shown that transaction costs could be reduced drastically and repayment rates can be as high as 90 per cent. Both RBI and National Bank for Agriculture and Rural Development (NABARD) have been spear-heading the promotion and linkage of SHGs to the banking system through refinance support and other proactive policies. Three models of credit linkage of SHGs with banks have emerged: (i) SHGs formed and financed by banks; (ii) SHGs formed by NGOs but directly financed by banks; and (iii) SHGs financed by banks using NGOs as financial intermediaries. The second model has emerged as the most popular model. Thus, the programme launched in 1992 has enabled the formal banking system to reach a large number of poor households through the conduit of 2 million credit-linked SHGs as at end-March 2006.

The role of microcredit as the most appropriate and economically feasible *modus operandi* in attaining the twin objectives of growth and poverty alleviation is thus well established and the rural credit system—commercial banks, cooperatives and RRBs—must move towards spreading this model and that too fast. The coverage of poor families today is modest. Also, in terms of regional distribution, there is uneven growth of MFIs. At the end of March 2003, of the total SHGs credit-linked with banks, Andhra Pradesh accounted for nearly 40 per cent. Taking four states Andhra Pradesh, Karnataka, Tamil Nadu and Uttar Pradesh together accounted for nearly 70 per cent of the SHGs credit-linked and 80 per cent of the total amount of bank loans. There is therefore the urgent need to replicate this model of reaching rural credit to different segments of the rural sector through the instrumentality of SHGs or NGOs in other states. Of course, NABARD has been playing a catalytic role both in terms of promotional grant support to NGOs and nurturing SHGs. But this is not enough. Public sector banks (PSBs), on thier part, should also make similar efforts to promote and nurture NGOs and SHGs: because such efforts will be mutually beneficial both to the lending institutions and the beneficiaries of bank credit. In order to give further boost to microfinance programme the Union Budget for 2006-07 announced several measures which included introduction of a Bill to provide a formal statutory framework for the promotion, development and regulation of microfinance sector, and advising NABARD to open a separate line of credit for financing farm production and investment activity through SHGs.

Banking Agents

Yet another model of linking NGOs and SHGs with banks has emerged with the RBI (2006b) issuing guidelines in February 2006. With the objective of extending savings and loan facilities to underprivileged and unbanked population, RBI has advised banks to use the services of NGOs,

SHGs, MFIs and other civil society organisations (CSOs) as intermediaries in providing financial and banking service. These intermediaries could act as business facilitators or correspondents. Commercial banks do not have to obtain RBI's prior approval for using these intermediaries as facilitators. How far this model would be effective in extending the reach of the banking system, time alone can demonstrate.

Concluding Comments

After experimenting with 'jobless growth' policies for the last 15 years or so, policymakers have now turned to 'inclusive growth', which is the new label for broad-based, decentralised growth. Inclusive growth in the real sector has become, in a way, a growth and development imperative. Growth, because high growth in GDP can be sustained only if sectors or segments of the economy which have become sluggish due to a number of factors including policy neglect, can be activated. Development, because inclusive growth is perhaps the only route by which large sections of the population, whom the growth process has bypassed, can be empowered to engage themselves in the growth process.

Financial inclusion can be regarded as a counterpart of inclusive growth in the real sector. Going by the official discourses on the subject, there seems to be a danger of financial inclusion being misconstrued as a 'credit security' on the analogy of 'food security'. We must guard ourselves against such danger. Availability of credit is, and will continue to be, limited and hence there has to be perforce, always a process of prioritisation, of preferential treatment, of selective extension of credit. Hence, for successful implementation of financial inclusion operation, the central bank would have to identify sectors or segments of the economy to which banks and other financial institutions should accord preferential treatment. In fact, the central bank should evolve region-specific profiles of baskets of such segments and persuade banks to ensure that their credit deployment is consistent with the priorities reflected in the basket. In terms of institutional reforms, the process of building the microcredit structure as an adjunct of the banking system should accelerate. In addition the central bank should put in place appropriate credit guarantee schemes, as also interest rate subsidisation schemes for credit flowing through microcredit institutions. Financial inclusion thus involves much more than mere numbers: only such a systemic perspective can make financial inclusion more meaningful.

References

Braun, Jochim Von, Ashok Gulati, and Shenggen Fan (2006). "Agricultural and Economic Development Strategies and the Transformation of China and India", *Annual Report, 2004-05,* Washington, D.C.: International Food Policy Research Institute.

Government of India (2006). Budget Speech of P. Chidambaram, Minister of Finance, Government of India, February 8, p. 11.

———. (2003). *Report of the Committee on Capital Formation in Agriculture*. New Delhi. March. p. 21.

Maxwell, Simon (2006). "What is Next in International Development?", *Working Paper* 270, London: Overseas Development Institute. June.

Mujumdar, N.A. (2006). "Centrality of Agriculture to India's Economic Development", *Economic and Political Weekly*. January 7.

———. (2004). *Economic Reforms Sans Development*. New Delhi: Academic Foundation.

———. (2001). *The New Architecture of the Rural Credit System*. Mumbai: Mumbai University.

Reddy, Y.V. (2006). *Annual Policy Statement for the Year 2006-07*. Mumbai: Reserve Bank of India. April. p. 56.

Reserve Bank of India (2006a). *Annual Report, 2005-06*. Mumbai. p. 2.

———. (2006b). *Monetary and Credit Information Review*. Mumbai. February.

Sen, Abhijit (2002). *Report of the High Level Committee on Long Term Grain Policy for the Country*. New Delhi: Ministry of Consumer Affairs, Food and Public Distribution.

Xiaoling, Wu (2004). "Promoting the Extension of Micro Credit", *BIS Review* 46.

Edited version of the address delivered on September 19, 2006 at Cochin, at the "National Conference of Financial Inclusion and Beyond: Issues and Opportunities for India", convened by the Institute of Small Enterprises and Development (ISED).

11 Rural Lending, Inclusive Growth and Financial Inclusion

Contemporary discourses on development clearly indicate that rural lending or rural credit generally, has today greatly metamorphosed from what it was say, in the 1950s—of the heydays of the famous All India Rural Credit Survey. Rural credit has now acquired new dimensions because of a number of factors. First, the inclusive growth strategy in the real sector embodied in the Eleventh Five-Year Plan (2007-2012) has important implications for rural credit policy (Mujumdar, 2007). Second, Reserve Bank of India (RBI), on its part, is pursuing vigorously its policy of financial inclusion. Already, 100 per cent financial inclusion is achieved in 28 districts in 8 states and the union territory of Puducherry. Are we seeking to treat 'credit security' on the analogy of 'food security'? If so, what happens to the viability of the lending institution and its governance? More basically, in the quest for 100 per cent financial inclusion are we not, in effect, dehyphenating credit and productive activities? These questions need to be raised before we chart out the future shape of the rural credit delivery system. Third, recognising the potential of microfinance to positively influence the upliftment of the poor, RBI has been making efforts to create an appropriate environment for its orderly development. In this context, the relationship of banks and microfinance institutions (MFIs) needs to be redefined. Fourth, it has become fashionable to argue, especially by some NGOs involved in microfinance, that the rural borrower does not mind paying a high rate of interest. What is important is the quantum and timeliness of credit. This is a dangerous proposition. Viability or profitability of an enterprise is as important in the case of rural borrowers as it is for urban borrowers. Financial sector reforms introduced in the 1990s seem to have been designed to pamper the private corporate sector and the net result has been the emergence of an inequitable interest rate structure, baised against agriculture and the rural borrowers. RBI's *Report on Currency and Finance 2005-06*, admits that, 'to compensate for sub-

BPLR lending, other segments are charged higher rates of interest, thus leading to cross subsidisation of economically well-off borrowers by the economically poor borrowers' (p. 159). Correcting this distortion is critical to the success of inclusive growth. Market theology should not be allowed to turn MFIs into glorified moneylenders. It is this new constellation of factors which would shape the future of rural credit.

Inclusive Growth in the Real Sector

'Inclusiveness' has really two dimensions: one in terms of sectors or segments of the economy which ought to be brought into the fold of a vibrant economy. Two, in terms of enabling sections of the population, whom the growth process has bypassed, to fully engage themselves with the development process.

In this context, the contemporary experience of China is illuminating. China, whose macroeconomic parameters were comparable to those of India, provides the most fascinating example of such inclusive growth. Today, China's manufacturing power is reshaping the world economy. The world capital-labour ratio has nearly halved because of the incorporation of its new labour force in the global economy. Analytically, what is important to highlight is that this impressive growth in manufacturing and even the double-digit growth in GDP sustained over more than two decades would not have been able, by themselves, to make a significant dent on the levels of unemployment or of poverty. It was the vibrant rural non-farm sector which played a critical role in the success story of drastically reducing poverty and unemployment. China's township and village enterprises (TVEs) provided increasing job opportunities outside agriculture, thereby argumenting household incomes. The phenomenal growth of this sector is demonstrated by the fact that its contribution to GDP rose to nearly one-third of total GDP in 2004, from practically zero in 1952. This has led to the creation of a whole new economic sector which became the most dynamic in the Chinese economy. The rural non-farm sector comprised, 'the small-scale food processing plants, machinery repair shops, and increasingly more modern and technologically intensive industries that cropped up to meet growing demand among increasingly well-off farmers and employ millions of people whose labour was no longer needed on farms' (Braun *et al.*, 2006).

Reverting to India, all those involved in development—banks, cooperatives, development finance institutions, NGOs and administrators at all levels—will have to rethink their own strategies in response to the new emphasis being given on 'inclusive growth'. Perhaps the first step in this direction is to identify the segments of the rural economy, on the analogy of the Chinese experience referred to above, which have so far not attracted adequate attention of policymakers but which have the potential to grow fast. As illustrative of the segments on which policy should focus, the following may be mentioned. Foremost among the sluggish sectors is agriculture which is central to India's economic development (Mujumdar, 2006). Agricultural growth decelerated from 3.1 per cent during the 1990s to 2.2 per cent in the Tenth Plan period. This could be attributed to declining public investments in agriculture and reduced flow of credit to agriculture. It has now been recognised that future agricultural growth will have to be necessarily water-centric. This is particularly so because more fertile lands like in the Punjab-Haryana region have perhaps reached a growth plateau. Apart from major irrigation works, five interconnected programmes, assume significance in this context: watershed development programme, both macro and micro; rain harvesting and conservation of water; renovation of traditional water bodies; improving water use efficiency in public irrigation works, notably in canals; and promotion of micro-irrigation technology, like drip and sprinkler irrigation systems.

The second bunch of projects is heterogeneous, encompassing diversification of agriculture like horticulture, floriculture, animal husbandry and fisheries. Then, there are land-related projects like development of wastelands and forests, soil conservation, drainage and flood control, organic farming with organic seed and compost preparation. Finally, a host of projects are connected with food processing, storage, warehousing and marketing.

The moot point is that the loan-portfolio of banks and other rural lending institutions must begin to reflect more diversified credit support to these emerging segments, and not merely support crop production, important though the latter will continue to be. The illustrative segments we have chosen to indicate above would offer projects which would be viable and hence eminently bankable.

It is obvious that inclusive growth is a far more complicated process, involving micro planning, evolving area-specific solutions and facilitating participation of a number of actors like Panchayati Raj Institutions (RPIs), state and Central governments, NGOs, SHGs etc.

Financial Inclusion

How should financial sector respond to this challenge of facilitating inclusive or broad-based and decentralised growth in the real sector? Is universal or 100 per cent financial inclusion, as the RBI seems to suggest the answer? I for one ask, would demur banking sector resources are, and would continue to be limited? Optimum utilisation of banking sector's resources would demand a selective approach to credit extension. Ideally, credit should follow productive activities and universal coverage would tantamount to dehyphenating credit and productive activities; and this does not augur well for facilitating inclusive growth. Of course, it is conceded that at present almost 40 per cent of the adult population of the country comprising mainly those with low incomes and those without collateral are unable to access mainstream financial products. And hence, capturing this section should be our long-term objective. In the meanwhile, if credit is made to chase productive activities, we would promote optimal use of banking sector resources. Spreading available resources too thinly, which universal coverage necessary implies, would not serve to optimise growth. Furthermore, opening 'no-frills' accounts with low charges would be reduced to mere tokenism. In fact, this may add to transaction costs and may provoke banks to raise their lending rates. The whole approach to universal financial coverage thus appears flawed and hence, second look at the issue is warranted.

Inequitable Interest: Rate Structure

I have all along argued that financial sector and banking sector reforms implemented in the 1990s have resulted in the emergence of an inequitable interest rate structure—a structure designed to pamper the private corporate sector and which is biased against agriculture and the small borrower (Mujumdar, 2002). For instance, there is no rationale for making a small farmer pay an interest rate of 12 per cent at a time when a highly rated corporate entity could raise money from banks at 6 per cent.

This paradoxical situation was the result of mindless implementation of Basel norms and adoption without adaptation concepts like 'risks' as understood in the developed world.

RBI's *Report on Currency and Finance 2005-06* provides valuable insights into the structure of interest rates; the low interest rate regime, it seems, was primarily designed to pamper the private corporate sector particularly the corporate elite. It was in April 2003 that the system of prime lending rates (PLRs) was replaced by a system of benchmark prime lending rates (BPLRs). However, the bulk of bank lending has been taking place at sub-BPLR rates; for instance, the share of sub-BPLR lending increased to 82 per cent by March 2007. While higher credit rated corporates are getting credit at sub-BPLR rates, agriculture and small scale industry (SSI) sectors and other small borrowers are generally charged BPLR or in some cases, above BPLR rates. The administered interest rate is applicable only in the case of agricultural loans below Rs. 2 lakh, short-term production credit upto Rs. 3 lakh, and export credit. According to the data of the *All India Debt and Investment Survey 2002*, about 82 per cent of rural debt was in the interest range of 12 to 20 per cent, while the PLRs of banks were in the region of 11 to 12 per cent. This raises several fundamental questions: 'to compensate for such sub-BPLR lending, other segments are charged higher rates of interest, thus leading to cross subsidisation of the economically well-off borrowers by the economically poor borrowers' (p. 159). It is gratifying to note that RBI has at long last conceded the point which some of us were making in the 1990s itself.

This is indeed disturbing, especially when the professed objective of both real sector growth in the Eleventh Plan and financial sector growth is to promote growth with equity. Why should the farmer pay an interest rate of 12 per cent, when the corporate elite could get away with paying only 6 per cent. Here again, the intellectual servility of Indian monetary policymakers of the 1990s to the market theology stands exposed. The ostensible reason for the farmer being made to pay a higher interest rate was that 'risks' involved in 'agricultural business' are greater than those involved in corporate lending. In any case, this is what standard textbooks by economists from the developed economies expound.

We must look at the problem from a broader perspective of the role of credit in a developing economy. In the Indian context, credit has a dual role: growth-enhancing and risk-reducing. Lending to agriculture, especially for purposes of reducing risks in agriculture, like a digging a well, or a bore-well, or even for rainwater harvesting and conservation, should attract a concessional interest rate. Because, at the same time as credit seeks to promote production, it also tends to reduce risks in the form of vulnerability to drought etc. It is thus clear that the 'received wisdom' about 'risks' is flawed (see Mujumdar, 2005).

In fact, in India it should be the medium-term objective of monetary and credit policies to seek to change the risk profile of the agricultural sector itself. Credit, both short-term and long-term, should be viewed in this context as a growth-enhancement and risk-reducing instrument. Obviously, the pricing of agricultural or rural credit in general will have to be quite different from the present method which is based entirely on 'received wisdom'.

Mechanistic application of market theology and mindless adoption of concepts from the developed world have led to the emergence of the present perverse interest rate structure which is inconsistent with inclusive growth in the real sector and financial inclusion. The approach to interest rate policy also reflects clearly a lack of appreciation of the centrality of agriculture and rural non-farm sector to India's economic development. One hopes that RBI addresses immediately the issue of correcting the present perverse interest rate structure.

Microfinance

Microfinance is expected to play an important role in promoting financial inclusion and inclusive growth. It is a sort of supplementary credit delivery system that is cost-effective and user-friendly for both banks and the poor borrowers. RBI's initiatives in promoting this channel of credit delivery have been centred around two models, namely SHG-bank linkage programme (SBLP) and the microfinance institutions (MFIs) model.

The SHG-Bank Linage Programme has remained the predominant microfinance model in the country. The total number of SHGs credit-linked to banks has reached 2.92 million. The phenomenal outreach of the programme has enabled 41 million poor households to gain access to microfinance from the formal banking system. The cumulative bank loans disbursed to SHGs upto March 2007 added upto Rs. 18,041 crore. The success of the programme has demonstrated its main advantages: timely repayment of loans to banks, reduction in transaction costs both to the poor borrowers and to banks, door-step saving and credit facility for the poor and exploitation of the untapped business potential of the rural sector. This programme needs to be expanded at a faster rate.

The government intends to promote MFIs in a big way. The corpus of Mirco Finance Development and Equity Fund (MFDEF) placed with NABARD was raised in 2005 to Rs. 200 crore from Rs. 100 crore.

At present, MFIs are functioning under various legal forms. A major area of concern is that many of them seek to charge very high rates of interest. There is no justification, particularly in the case of privately owned MFIs to charge exorbitant interest rates at, say, 30 or 35 per cent. It is ironical that government authorities go out of the way to exhort banks to maintain a low interest regime for the private corporate sector; but the same authorities wink at MFIs charging very high rates to small borrowers in the rural sector. This ambivalence needs to be corrected.

Of course, microcredit institutions must make profits to grow and remain viable. But there should be no 'profiteering' in the sense in which moneylenders have been traditionally operating in India. Viewed against this background, an interest rate of 30 per cent and above is far from justifiable. Textbooks of my generation on the Indian economy were fond of quoting M.L. Darling's statement (1925) that the Indian peasant is 'born in debt, lives in debt and dies in debt'. In the name of market theology, let us not perpetuate the Darling syndrome.

One final word about microfinance. We should treat this channel as a transit platform, the eventual objective being to facilitate the graduation of all these borrowers to the mainstream banking finances.

Concluding Comments

These three recent developments—inclusive growth strategy in the real sector, RBI's policy of financial inclusion, and the emergence of MFIs—have begun to change the profile of rural credit. All those involved in rural finance will have therefore to harmonise their lending policies, practices and procedures with the new profile. RBI, on its part, would do well to take a second look at the interest rate structure and also at its basic approach to financial inclusion.

References

Braun, Jochim Von, Ashok Gulari and Shenggen Fan (2006). "Agricultural and Economic Development Strategies and Transformation of China and India", *Annual Report 2004-05*. Washington, D.C.: International Food Policy Research Institute.

Darling, M.L. (1925). *The Punjab Peasant in Prosperity and Debt*. Oxford. pp.58-59.

Mujumdar, N.A. (2007). *Inclusive Growth: Development Perspectives in Indian Economy*. New Delhi: Academic Foundation.

———. (2006). "Centrality of Agriculture to India's Economic Development", *Economic and Political Weekly*. January 7.

———. (2005). "Risk Philosophy: An Enquiry into Risks and Uncertainties in Agriculture and the Role of Credit", *Occasional Paper* 41. Mumbai: Development of Economic Analysis and Research, NABARD.

———. (2002). *Financial Sector Reforms and India's Economic Development* (2 Vols.). New Delhi: Academic Foundation.

12 Next Generation Financial Sector Reforms and Inclusive Growth

The Eleventh Five-Year Plan (2007-2012) is based on the strategy of inclusive growth that is, broad-based and decentralised growth. If the growth in the real sector has to be not only higher but also more inclusive, what kind of financial engineering is required—in terms of institutional framework, financial instruments and lending procedures and practices—to facilitate more such inclusive growth? The Planning Commission, in August 2007, appointed a High Level Committee on Financial Sector Reforms (CFSR) with, among others, the following terms of reference:

To identify the emerging challenges in meeting the financing needs of the Indian economy in the coming decade and to identify real sector reforms that would allow those needs to be more easily met by the financial sector. The draft report of the committee is now in the public domain (GoI, 2008).

The high profile nature of the Committee is reflected not only in the composition of the Committee but also in its terms of reference. Headed by Prof. Raghuram Rajan, at the 12 member team included K.V. Kamath of the ICICI, O.P. Bhatt of the State Bank of India, and Udaya Kotak of Kotak Mahindra Bank. The conspicuous absence of a representative from Reserve Bank of India (RBI) may make one wonder whether the Committee had any hidden agenda! The terms of reference, were equally impressive: to provide an outline of 'the next generation of financial sector reforms' (Ibid.: 1).

While there are so many reports on different segments of financial sector—for instance, Dr. Vaidyanathan's Report on the cooperative credit institutions (2009) and Dr. Rangarajan's Report on Financial Inclusion (2008)—this Report was expected to paint a broader canvass of the entire financial sector. The Report claims to attempt to 'see links that others have not' and to create mutually reinforcing influences in the financial sector. The Committee puts forward its proposals for financial reform with a threefold objective: to foster growth itself, to include more Indians in the growth process; and to improve financial stability (GoI, 2008: 2). The third objective has become important in the contemporary situation when the subprime crisis has engulfed many developed countries and has threatened to spill over to some emerging economies. The Committee does not make a secret of its high profile nature in the sense that it does not suffer from the traditional virtue of scholarly work, namely 'modesty'. Take the following statement: '...practical pieces of legislation that seem to be exempt from any intellectual influence, are usually drawn from some long forgotten report. Despite the current political climate this is indeed the reason we have no doubt this report will not be a wasted report' (Ibid.: 5).

This Report indeed covers a wide range of issues: the future role of RBI, a national goal of ensuring in three years that 90 per cent of households have access to a deposit account, allowing entry of more private well-governed small finance banks, modifying priority sector mandate, discontinuing government ownership of banks, by selling small under performing public sector banks, promote exchange rate derivatives, establishment of financial ombudsman, and so on. More importantly the Committee believes in taking a hundred small steps towards reforms. 'Instead of focusing primarily on a few large and usually politically controversial steps, we need to take a hundred small steps in the same direction that will collectively take us very far' (Ibid.: 3). We will have occasion to discuss later such selective small steps recommended by the Committee.

This Report needs to be analysed in depth because of the following two reasons. First, in view of its high profile nature there is the danger that government may accept its major recommendations, some of which may have far reaching implications for the economy. Unfortunately, most of these recommendations are based on an amateurish understanding of the Indian economy and hence, if implemented, they may prove counter-productive. Second, the Committee has failed to address the basic issue we raised at the beginning: how to reshape the financial system with a view to promote more inclusive growth?

This Report belongs to the genre of IMF/World Bank Reports, characterised by excellent presentation, obsessed with market theology and marked by a sense of superciliousness. The Report embodies doctrinaire policy prescriptions inspired by pure market theology, and not rooted in the India-specific socioeconomic milieu. To borrow a phrase from the Committee's Report—'market theology overtakes reasoned debate'. The authors of the Report lack a sense of Indian economic history and have presented their recommendations in the form of a series of *obiter dicta* rather than as recommendations emerging from analyses of empirical data or experience. They seem to have been carried away, as it were, by the rhetorics of international best practices. The bulk of the recommendations lack intellectual support. The Committee's commitment to market theology has eclipsed all other commitments like commitment to enlarge employment opportunities or reduce poverty. Finally, the random assortment of proposals for financial sector reforms lack the vision to portray the kind of financial structure we need to aim to build. Some core issues, as we will discuss later, involved in the transfiguration of the financial sector, with a view to enabling it to facilitate inclusive growth in the real sector, have been conveniently bypassed.

Privatisation, liberalisation, independent central banks focussing exclusively on inflation control, non-intervention by government in the agricultural sector—these are some of the essential ingredients of neo-liberalism—neo-classical market fundamentalism that underlay the so-called 'Washington Consensus'. And this market fundamentalism is, writ large on the Committee's Report. The Committee should have realised that countries which followed this ideology have been disillusioned by empirical experience. Pragramatic economists and multilateral financial institutions are already discarding this thesis.

In fact this question forms part of a larger issue of the changing face of development economics itself. As Prof. John Humphery (2007) puts it:

> Historically, much development thinking assumes the superiority of, or at least the dominance of the West. The rise of Asia shows that new economies are the global success stories and their expansion is shaping growth and development...New multiple Southern policy agendas—backed up by financial muscle, the credibility that goes with rapid growth, an intellectual and policy making capacity—are forcing a reinvention of development studies.

One would have thought that the High Level Committee would at least seek to reinvent, in the sense mentioned by Prof. Humphery, the financial system which would be best able to promote inclusive growth in the real sector. Instead, the Committee is content with merely recommending the mimicking of the systems or institutions of the West. I have made an exploratory attempt to draw a blueprint of the kind of financial system we need to build, if the objective of inclusive growth in the real sector is to achieved: the need to integrate banks, microfinance institutions (MFIs), self-help groups (SHGs) and non-government organisations (NGOs) (see Mujumdar, 2007).

Congenital Dislike of Public Sector

Congenital dislike of public sector is an integral part of the IMF/World bank philosophy. This Report reflects faithfully this theology: 'The majority of this Committee does not see a compelling reason for continuing government ownership. There are other activities where government attention and resources are more important. However, the Committee does recognise that public opinion in this country is divided on the issue of privatisation. A parallel approach is to undertake reforms that would remove constraints on the public sector banks, even while retaining government ownership. Intermediate steps such as reducing the government ownership below 50 per cent while retaining its control (as suggested by the Narasimham Committee) are possible' (GoI, 2008: 10). The Committee has therefore recommended, to begin with, 'sell small under performing public sector banks, possibly to another bank or to a strategic investor to gain experience with the process and gauge outcomes' (Ibid.: 11).

This doctrinaire prescription shows that the Committee is innocent of the recent financial history of India. The branch expansion programme in the post-nationalisation period (post-1969) was unprecedented in the history of world banking. In retrospect one could see the widening and deepening of the Indian banking system as a process of modernisation of the Indian economy (Mujumdar, 2002). Only the public banking system and directed credit policy could have achieved these goals. No private sector banks would even think in terms of such goals. The history of banking in former British colonies like say, Zambia or South Africa provides enough evidence of this statement. And all this was achieved in India well before the concept of 'financial inclusion' became fashionable.

Ironically, the High Level Committee also advocates 'a national goal of ensuring in 3 years that 90 per cent of the households, if they so desire, have access to a deposit account and to a payment system' (GoI, 2008: 7). It would be naive to expect private sector banks, either domestic or foreign, to address this issue.

After the implementation of banking sector reforms in 1990, including the Basel norms, the Indian banking system has become 'strong and sound', as Pai (2007), a professional banker has demonstrated, with all the relevant data. 'The banks have been able to show strong balance sheet growth in the post-reforms period in an environment of operational flexibility. Improvement in the financial health of banks is reflected in the improvement in capital Adequacy and Asset Quality. This progress has been achieved despite the adoption of international best practices and prudential norms and renewing out goals of social banking *viz.*, maintaining wide reach of banking system and directing credit towards important disadvantaged sections of the Society.'

Thus it is to the credit of the Indian banking policymakers that they have been able to successfully blend the objectives of social banking with the market theology of maximising profitability of banks. Where is then the case for privatisation?

While on this subject, we may also consider the Committee's other recommendation that small private sector banks should be allowed to be set up and the minimum capital requirement could be reduced significantly from the present minimum of Rs. 300 crore (GoI, 2008: 8).

This proposal also shows that the Committee is innocent of history of Indian banking. Visceral memories of the, pre-1960, mushrooming of small banks of indifferent quality should sound a note of warning. During the post-war period 1946 to 1950, 207 banks with paid up capital of Rs. 5.33 crore had failed. It was really the failure of Laxmi Bank and Palai Central Bank in 1960 which triggered RBI's action to weed out a large number of unviable commercial banks. Through a process of moratorium and merger the number of scheduled commercial banks was reduced to about 100.

More recently, some not-so-viable, small, private sector banks had to seek shelter under public sector banks: Lord Krishna Bank merged with the Punjab National Bank, Global Trust with Oriental Bank of Commerce, and United Western Bank with the IDBI bank. The Committee should have realised that banking efficiency is ownership neutral i.e., reform of the public sector banks? yes; their total elimination? no.

Reserve Bank of India

Let us now turn to another major recommendation of the Committee relating to the future role of RBI. First, the Committee seems to have set out to cut the RBI to size, for no rhyme or reason. 'The RBI should formally have a single objective, to stay close to a low inflation number, or within a range, in the medium term and more steadily to a single instrument, the short-term interest rate (repo and reverse repo) to achieve it' (Ibid.: 5). This recommendation would have made sense if the Committee had demonstrated with the necessary data and empirical evidence that RBI had failed to contain inflation because it had pursued multiple objectives. It has not even attempted this exercise. On the contrary, RBI's track record in this area is excellent. Taking more recent years, inflation decelerated from an average of 10.3 per cent between 1991-1994 to 8.9 per cent between 1995-1999 and to 4.3 per cent during the current decade. Equally important is the fact that the regime of inflation control has, in turn, stabilised inflation expectations. In fact RBI has further lowered the 'policy tolerance threshold' from 4 to 4.5 per cent to around 3 per cent, as a medium-term objective.

Parenthetically, one must add that the alarm regarding inflation reaching 11 per cent during the current financial year 2008-09 is an aberration brought out primarily by external factors like the international oil prices soaring to unprecedented levels. It has not much to do with RBI's capability of controlling inflation.

In terms of instruments also, if RBI has been able to use a mix of instruments to successfully rein in inflation, why should it restrict its operations to a single instrument? The Committee's recommendation lacks intellectual support.

Basically, central banks in developing countries or even in emerging economies have to play a developmental role. That is why the founding fathers of RBI built into its statute, the responsibility of developing the infrastructure for rural credit. As we have spelt out earlier, historically, RBI has played an active role in widening and deepening of the banking system.

Even at the current juncture, financial inclusion has become a pre-condition for promoting inclusive growth in the real sector. Ironically, the Committee itself has, as we have mentioned earlier, set a target for wider banking coverage of the population. Given these objectives, to restrict RBI's function to 'one objective, one instrument' regime hardly makes any sense.

The Committee makes another textbookish recommendation: RBI should cease to manage the exchange rate of the rupee and should be 'intervening in currency markets only to limit excessive volatility' (GoI, 2008: 5). The Committee believes that, given capital flows, 'the real exchange rate, which is the key factor determining India's competitiveness, is influenced by factors such as productivity growth and demand supply imbalances that are not changed by central bank intervention against the dollar' (Ibid.: 5). In the real world, we all know, managed currency is the rule rather than an exception. The contemporary example is China whose monetary authorities refuse to up-value its currency *vis-à-vis* dollar, despite pressures from the US. Historically, Japan also followed a similar policy. Leaving the exchange rate to be solely determined by market forces is a sure recipe for disaster. Speculative capital flows can play havoc with exchange rates.

Warehouse Receipts and Bill Market Schemes

Among the random assortment of recommendations of the Committee two rather minor recommendations may be briefly discussed. First, 'trading of warehouse receipts'. To quote: 'With the promulgation expected soon of the Warehousing (Development and Regulation) Act, 2008, warehouse receipts will become a negotiable instrument: They will become a new reliable form of collateral in the agricultural sector, where till now there was no other security except land, which has its own infirmities. ...Warehouse receipts can be in physical or electronical form and must be issued by registered warehouses which will be accredited by the

Warehousing Development and Regulating Authority' (GoI, 2008: 3). Further, the Committee proclaims grandiloquently: 'Assuming that at any time, about 11-20 per cent of the annual agricultural produce is stored in warehouses, the Act has the potential to inject over US $30 billion of agricultural credit' (Ibid.: 3). The unwary reader may be led to believe that this instrument is the 'discovery' of the Committee. But those who are familiar with the recent economic history of India, however, would point out that the warehouse receipts issue dates back to the recommendations of the famous All-India Rural Credit Survey (1956). If the Committee were serious, they should have investigated why warehouse receipts, as a financial instrument, have failed to gain wider acceptance during these 50 years and what should be done to remove the impediments which come in the way of popularising the instrument. The Committee did not condescend to undertake such an exercise.

A similar homily is reflected in their recommendations relating to small and medium industries. 'As another example, credit to small and medium enterprises could be boosted enormously if the trade receivable claims they have on large firms could be converted to electronic format accepted by large firms and sold as commercial paper' (Ibid.: 3). If the Committee had cared to study the efforts made by RBI in the past in this area, it would have been in a position to go beyond this textbook recommendation. RBI had even tried to make it mandatory for large firms to clear their dues to small industries as part of the conditionality of access to bank credit. There were also several aborted efforts of RBI to promote the Bill market schemes. But the Committee did not condescend to examine why these schemes failed to take off.

Absence of Intellectual Macro Framework

The trouble with the Committee is that there is no intellectual macro framework against which its main recommendations have been formulated. This has led to several internal inconsistencies, disjointed recommendations, and failure to identify the basic issues. Let us take three examples. First, focus on rural areas. 'In addition, this Committee would suggest moving away from a sole focus on rural areas, where undoubtedly many of our poor live, to also include the urban areas, where, more of them are migrating' (GoI, 2008: 7). In contrast, the Committee asserts elsewhere '... Indeed the road to making Mumbai an international financial centre runs through every village and slum in India' (Ibid.: 21).

Second, the Committee is against concessional interest rates to the poor. 'Liberalising interest rates would allow the formal sector to lend to the poor and keep them from the moneylender, though liberalisation would require the political will to accept the widespread evidence that low interest rate ceilings simply do not help the poor' (Ibid.: 9). This reflects an amateurish understanding of the rural realities. Even the World Bank, the fountain head of market theology, has now accepted the thesis that concessional lending is essential at least initially, to facilitate the poor escape from the poverty trap. The Committee did not bother to examine why the present interest rate structure in India is inequitable, biased against the low-income borrowers.

The third point pertains to the very rationale of why inclusive growth in the real sector has become necessary. Here the Committee exposes its innocence: 'Ultimately, though it is opportunities in the real sector, created by broader growth, which will give the poor the ability to use credit effectively. Instead of forcing credit to household that could thereby become heavily indebted, the focus should be on making them credit-worthy so that when opportunities arise, they have access' (Ibid.: 7).

Basically inclusive growth in the real sector has now become a growth and development imperative: growth because a high GDP growth like 8 or 9 per cent targeted in the Eleventh Plan (2007-2012) can be sustained only if other sectors or segments of the economy, which have been sluggish because of a number of reasons, including policy neglect, can be activated. Development, because this is perhaps the best route by which the bulk of the poor can be provided with livelihood and food security (Mujumdar, 2007). In other words, we can no longer depend on 'autonomous' forces for growth of the real sector; this growth has to be policy-induced with a view to enabling sections of the population, whom the growth process has bypassed, to fully engage themselves with the development process. An interventionist and proactive policy is therefore warranted. This should be the starting point for designing what the Committee calls 'the next generation financial sector reforms'. In this context, the contemporary experience of China is illuminating. China's township and village enterprises (TVEs) provided increasing job opportunities outside agriculture and this phenomenal expansion of non-farm sector played a critical role in reducing poverty.

Three Core Issues

In the contemporary financial scenario in India, there are three core issues: (i) broad-based, decentralised growth in the real sector, (ii) the new architecture of the financial system to facilitate such growth, and (iii) the inequitable interest rate structure. Logically, the reinvention of the next generation financial sector reforms should have emerged from a holistic analysis of these three core issues. Judged by these criteria, the Committee has frittered away its energies on a random assortment of recommendations: some relevant, some not so relevant, many aimed at mimicking the 'best practices' of banking in the developed world. Thus the Report has acquired the characteristics of a PhD thesis: prolixity and discursiveness. The Committee has not done its homework on the economic realities at the ground level, as the ensuring discussion would demonstrate.

First, the unorganised sector holds the key to broad-based decentralised growth. The recent Report on the sector spells out that microenterprises—an investment of below Rs. 0.5 million—constitute 94 per cent of small enterprises in the country and provide employment to 70 million people and contribute 30 per cent of industrial production. Despite occupying this central position these enterprises receive only 2 per cent of net bank credit (GoI, 2007). If additional credit is injected into this sector it may lead not only to higher production, but it may also promote upgradation of technology, improvement in marketing efficiency, and so on.

With the growing importance of small and medium-sized enterprises (SMEs), the credit delivery system needs to be streamlined. For instance, since there is no or little information about such SMEs credit history, banks are prone to insist on collateral for their advances to this segment. The goal of collateral—free lending both for microenterprises and SMEs seems to be far away.

Second, the institutional infrastructure. Microfinance is expected to play an important role in promoting financial inclusion and inclusive growth. It is a sort of supplementary credit delivery system that is cost-effective and user-friendly for both banks and the poor borrowers. RBI's initiatives in promoting this channel of credit delivery have centred around two models, namely SHG-Bank Linkage programme and microfinance institutions (MFI) model (Mujumdar, 2008). At the same time, the cooperative credit structure is being reorganised on the lines recommended by the Vaidyanathan Committee. Similarly, the more recent developments reveal that regional rural banks (RRBs) could become the main institutional mechanism for providing credit to the poor. As Dr. Thingalaya (2007), a professional banker puts it: 'The process of their merger at the state level, reducing the number from 196 to 96 has expanded their operational base considerably. The best among them like the Karnataka Vikas Grameen Bank or Pragathi Grameen Bank are comparable to the best grameen bank, anywhere in the world, including the much publicised banks of Bangladesh... Out of the 1.29 crore of borrowing accounts handled by them, 1.07 crore or 83 per cent are in the advances group of less than Rs. 25,000.'

The blueprint for the future institutional structure should clearly indicate how the pyramid comprising banks, RRBs, cooperatives, MFIs and SHGs needs to be built.

Finally, the inequitable interest rate structure. The Committee's pontification on why the concessional lending rates do not help the poor further exposes its innocence of the realities of the present interest rate structure. Financial sector and banking sector reforms implemented in the 1990s have resulted in the emergence of an inequitable interest rate structure, a structure designed to pamper the private corporate sector, and which is biased against agriculture and the small borrower generally. For instance, a small farmer was made to pay an interest rate of 12 per cent at a time when a highly rated corporate entity could raise money from banks at 6 per cent (Mujumdar, 2002). This paradoxical situation was the result of mindless implementation of Basel norms and adoption without adaptation concept like 'risks' as understood in the developed world. RBI *Report on Currency and Finance, 2005-06* provides valuable insights into the structure of interest rates. The bulk of bank lending has been taking place at sub-BPLR (benchmark prime lending rate). For instance, the share of sub-BPLR lending increased to 82 per cent by March 2007. While higher credit rated corporates are getting credit at sub-BPLR rates, agriculture, small industry and other small borrowers are generally charged BPLR, or in some cases, above BPLR rates. To quote the RBI Report: 'to compensate for such sub-BPLR lending, other segments are charged higher rates of interest, thus leading to cross subsidisation of the economically well-off borrowers by the economically poor borrowers' (2006: 159). This is indeed disturbing especially when the objective of both the inclusive growth in the real sector as envisaged in the Eleventh Plan and financial inclusion is to promote growth with equity. The next generation financial reforms must address this question.

In this context, it is important to highlight that the World Bank—the citadel of market theology—has itself changed its attitude to concessional lending and support systems to poor farmers or poor borrowers generally. As Jeffrey Sachs (2008) has pointed out recently, during the debt crisis of the 1980s and 1990s, both the IMF and World Bank forced dozens of poor food-importing countries to dismantle their state support systems, including concessional lending to the poor farmers. Poor farmers were told to fend for themselves, to let market forces provide for farm inputs. Empirical experience showed that this proved counterproductive. Under its new president, Robert Zoellick, the World Bank has now stepped forward to provide grants to state governments to establish the support systems, including concessional lending, for poor farmers to enable them to gain access to inputs like seeds fertiliser and irrigation. One would wish that the Committee should have updated itself with these new developments in market theology, before offering their advice on interest rates.

Overall, any blueprint for the next generation financial sector reforms can be meaningful only if it addresses these three core issues.

References

Government of India (2008). *Draft Report of the Committee on Financial Sector Reforms* (CFSR). Planning Commission. April.

———. (2007). *Report on Conditions of Work and Promotion of Livelihoods in the Unorganised Sector*. p.221.

Humphrey, John (2007). "Asian Drivers: China, India and Development", in *Moving Towards 360 Degree Research IDS Annual Report, 2006-07*. University of Sussex, Brighton.

Mujumdar, N.A. (2008). "Rural Lending, Inclusive Growth and Financial Inclusion", *The Journal of the Indian Institute of Banking and Finance*. January-March.

———. (2007). *Inclusive Growth: Development Perspectives in Indian Economy*. New Delhi: Academic Foundation.

———. (2002). *Financial Sector Reforms and India's Economic Development* (2 Volumes), New Delhi: Academic Foundation.

Pai, D.T. (2007). *Overview of Banking Development, 1947-2007*. Manipal. p.111.

RBI (2006). *Report on Currency and Finance, 2005-06*, Mumbai: Reserve Bank of India. p.159.

Thingalaya, N.K. (2007). "Annals of a Central Bank" *Indian Economic Journal.* April-June.

Sachs, D. Jeffrey. (2008). "A New Deal for Poor Farmers", *Economic Times*, May 23.

This paper is a contribution to the Volume being brought out to felicitate Professor S.L.N. Simha, former Economic Adviser, Reserve Bank of India, on his completion of 90 years.

Part III

Monetary and Credit Policies

13 Monetary and Credit Policies in the Post-Reforms Period

An Assessment

The broad objectives of monetary policy have continued to remain, in the post-reforms phase, the same as before. The twin objectives are: maintaining a reasonable degree of price stability, and ensuring adequate flow of credit to the productive sectors of the economy.[1] The opening up of the Indian economy as a consequence of reforms, has added a new dimension to monetary management. 'While monetary policy has operated reasonably well on the domestic demand-supply and credit deposit balances even as liquidity emanating from capital flows has been absorbed in the short-term, the key future challenge is liquidity management, taking into account the current level of capital flows. The persistence of these flows has implications for domestic financial stability and future inflation with potential lagged effects on aggregate demand. Consequently, monetary policy will have to address not only the liquidity overhand but also incremental flows on future if they continue at present levels' (Reddy, 2007c: 56).

As we will see, monetary expansion in the last couple of years was mainly driven by sizeable accretion to net foreign exchange assets. Even during the current financial year 2007-08 for instance, forex reserves have risen by more than $91 billion (up to February 8, 2008). Money supply (M_3) expansion at 16.5 per cent during the current year so far was higher than the 14 per cent expansion recorded during the corresponding period of 2006-07. This is a phenomenon common to many emerging market economies (EMEs). Central bankers in these countries are steeped into issues of large capital flows and their impact on monetary policy. New instruments to tackle this problem have been forged: in India, issuance of

1. For an excellent official discourse on monetary policy see: Reddy (2007a and 2007b).

securities under the market stabilisation scheme (MSS) and operations under liquidity adjustment facility (LAF). Thus monetary policy will have to address not only liquidity overhang but also incremental flows.

There is a fourth dimension which is India-specific, namely the new objective of financial inclusion. Following the recommendations of the *Report of the Committee on Financial Inclusion*, supply-led expansion in credit is envisaged (Rangarajan, 2008). The National Rural Financial Inclusion Plan (NRFIP) stipulates that an additional 55.77 million households would be covered through rural and semi-urban branches of commercial banks and regional rural banks (RRBs) by 2012. The target is that 250 new cultivators and non-cultivators would be added per branch per annum. Such universal financial inclusion or 100 per cent coverage of households has already been achieved in 28 districts and in Puducherry. This approach of universal coverage raises issues of optimal use of banking sectors' resources and also its impact on GDP growth.

I would seek to discuss the monetary and credit policies pursued in the post-reforms period in the framework of these four parameters.

Inflation Control

While assessing the performance of monetary policy it can be said without hesitation that it has succeeded in achieving the key objective of controlling inflation. In respect of the second objective of facilitating growth, however it seems to have floundered. Inflation as measured by the wholesale price index (WPI) has decelerated from an average of 10.3 per cent between 1990-1994, to 8.9 per cent between 1995-1999 and to 4.3 per cent during the current decade. Equally important is the fact that the regime of moderate inflation has, in turn, stabilised inflation expectations. In fact, what Reserve Bank of India (RBI) terms as the 'policy tolerance threshold', seems to have been further lowered. While setting the inflation target at 5 per cent for 2007-08, RBI makes the following significant statement: 'In recognition of India's evolving integration with the global economy and societal preferences in this regard, the resolve, going forward, would be to condition expectations in the range of 4.0–4.5 per cent so that an inflation rate of around 3 per cent becomes a medium-term objective consistent with India's broader integration into the global economy' (Reddy, 2007c: 64).

Such deceleration in inflation in India is not an isolated experience but seems to have been part of a broader global phenomenon of what is termed the 'Great Moderation'—the sustained decline in the volatility of output and inflation. Prof. Kenneth Rogoff of Harvard University has argued that improved competitiveness as a result of globalisation coupled with better policies has had a major positive impact on inflationary trend in many countries (Mboweni, 2007). However, the impact of globalisation on inflation in India needs an in-depth study.

Growth Story

Let us now track the growth story, or, extending adequate credit support to productive sectors. Analytically, it is convenient to divide the post-reforms period into two distinct phases: the period 1991 to 2004, which can be categorised as an 'era of exclusion'; and the period subsequent to 2004—which can be termed as a phase of 'return to inclusion'. The first phase was a market theology phase, when the Indian monetary policymakers appeared to be intoxicated with undiluted market theology of the IMF and the World Bank. A number of policy mistakes were committed: the flow of credit to agriculture, and priority sectors generally, decelerated and a large number of small farmers, or small borrowers generally, were thrown out of the banking systems. The rural credit delivery system was allowed to become moribund. An inequitable interest rate structure emerged which was biased against the small borrowers and in favour of the corporate elite of the private sector. For instance, while a highly rated corporate entity could raise money from banks at say 6 per cent, the small farmers continued to pay an interest rate of 12 per cent. Mindless implementation of Basel norms, which the banking sector reforms boiled down to, bred a new banking culture which shunned lending to agriculture, or small scale industries (SSIs) and which focussed on lending to the three 'Cs'—corporate elite, consumer durables and capital market related activities. No wonder that agricultural growth decelerated to lower than 2 per cent in 1990s (See Mujumdar, 2002).

Happily, all this is changing on the eve of the Eleventh Plan. Indian policymakers seem to have gone through a process of intellectual transformation to realise that moving away from undiluted market theology is essential to ensure that the development content of growth does not wither away. The Eleventh Five-Year Plan (2007-2012) itself is based on a strategy of inclusive growth in the real sector, that is broad-based decentralised growth. The RBI on its part, has responded promptly to this change. The quantum of bank credit flow to agriculture doubled during the three-year period (2004-2007). RBI is pursuing vigorously its policy of financial inclusion: already 100 per cent inclusion has been achieved in 28 districts and in Puducherry. Bank-SHGs linkage programme is being given a push and microcredit institutions are being actively promoted. Thus, 2004 marks a departure from the stance of monetary and credit policies followed in the first phase and represents a 'return to inclusion'.

One conspicuous example of mindless implementation of banking sector reforms based on market theology casuing harm to the Indian economy may be cited here. In the euphoria of financial sector reforms directed credit was shunned and hence the Narasimham Committee which set the agenda for banking sector reforms, had recommended that the credit target for priority sectors be reduced from 40 per cent of net bank credit to 10 per cent. Of course, RBI did not accept this recommendation in principle but in practice banks defaulted on credit targets both in respect of credit to agriculture (18 per cent) and priority sectors (40 per cent). RBI winked at these defaults.

These reformers lacked the macro vision of the India-specific situation. Though the share of agriculture in total GDP is declining steadily over the years and now accounts for some 20 per cent of GDP, what is important to underline is that about 60 per cent of the population continues to depend on agriculture. In contrast to the empirical experience of developed countries, there has been no siphoning off of surplus population away from the agricultural sector. Enhanced growth of the agricultural sector thus becomes imperative for ensuring food security, poverty alleviation, price stability, overall inclusive growth and sustainability of higher growth of the economy. The centrality of agriculture to India's economic development needs to be recognised (Mujumdar, 2006).

Secondly, inflationary pressures have re-emerged as a key risk to global growth. In the global food market, prices of major crops such as corn, soyabeans and wheat have risen by end-December 2007, by 22.4 per cent, 75.2 per cent and 87.7 per cent, respectively from a year ago, in response to surging demand. The FAO's global food price index (FPI) rose by 40 per cent in 2007—to the highest level on record. In the global coarse grain market also prices have risen, driven by strong demand for animal feed as well as for ethanol: 'More recently, food prices have jumped sharply, at least in part because of an attempt to encourage the use of the so-called bio-fuels in industrial countries (Johnson, 2007). Central banks, even in developed countries have now realised that food prices have a significant impact on inflation expectations—a parameter which is vital for the conduct of monetary policy. This aspect is particularly significant in developing economies like India because the weightage for food prices in the price index is very large.

The belated recognition of these dimensions perhaps explains the change in the stance of monetary and credit policies in India in the post-2004 phase.

Reverting to the growth story, the performance of the economy is excellent. Real GDP growth during the Tenth Plan period (2002-03 to 2006-07) averaged 7.6 per cent—the highest average growth during any Plan period so far. If we take the most recent three years 2005-06, 2006-07 and 2007-08, the average growth works out to nearly 9 per cent. What is then the matter for concern? It is the growth that has been skewed, or, to use the currently fashionable word, not 'inclusive', with some sectors like agriculture being excluded from the high growth performers. The centrality of agriculture to India's economic growth means that the benefits of growth have bypassed a large sections of the population. Inclusive growth has thus become both a growth and a development imperative: growth because a high GDP growth can be sustained only if other sectors or segments of the economy, which have been sluggish because of a number of factors, including policy neglect, can be activated; development, because this is perhaps the best route by which the bulk of the poor can be provided with livelihood and food security (Mujumdar, 2007). Facilitating inclusive growth, or broad-based decentralised growth in the real sector adds a new dimension to the objectives of monetary and credit policy. RBIs recent efforts to promote financial inclusion could be interpreted as response of monetary authorities to the new claims made on it.

If one of the objectives of monetary policy is to facilitate faster growth of GDP, it becomes imperative to focus on unmet demand for credit by productive activities. In the hierarchy of priorities, this should claim the first place.

We must look at the problem from a broader perspective of the role of credit in a developing economy. In the Indian context, credit has a dual role: growth-enhancing and risk reducing. Lending to agriculture, especially for purposes of reducing risks in agriculture, like a digging a well, or a bore-well, or even for rain water harvesting and conservation, should attract a concessional interest rate. Because, at the same time as credit seeks to promote production, it also rends to reduce risks in the form of vulnerability to drought, etc. It is thus clear that the 'received wisdom' about 'risks' is flawed. I have examined this whole issue thoroughly in the Monograph prepared for NABARD (Mujumdar, 2005).

In fact in India it should be the medium-term objective of monetary and credit policies to seek to change the risk profile of the agricultural sector itself. Credit, both short-term and long-term, should be viewed in this context as a growth-enhancement and risk-reducing instrument. Obviously, the pricing of agricultural or rural credit in general, will have to be quite different from the present method which is based entirely on 'received wisdom'.

Mechanistic application of market theology and mindless adoption of concepts from the developed world have led to the emergence of the present perverse interest rate structure which is inconsistent with inclusive growth in the real sector and financial inclusion. The approach to interest rate policy also reflects clearly a lack of appreciation of the centrality of agriculture and rural non-farm sector to India's economic development. One hopes that RBI addresses immediately the issue of correcting present perverse interest rate structure.

Runaway Expansion of Bank Credit

Another worrying feature of banking developments is the runaway expansion of bank credit witnessed in recent-years: non-food credit expanded by an annual average rate of 30 per cent during the three years (2003-2006). This runaway expansion has to be contextualised. First, robust macroeconomic performance continued to underpin the performance of banks. GDP accelerated to 9.4 per cent in 2006-07 from 9 per cent in the previous year. Real GDP growth during the Tenth Plan period (2002-03 to 2006-07) averaged 7.6 per cent—the highest average rate of growth during any Plan period so far. Second, banks could sustain such an unprecedented growth in credit because they had built up surplus liquidity in the form of excess investments in SLR (statutory liquidity ratio) securities. By bringing down their surplus resources banks have been able to sustain such a phenomenal expansion in credit. This is clear from the fact the incremental credit-deposit ratio was as high as 110 per cent at end-March 2006 and this ratio declined to 81 per cent at end-March 2007. The ratio was thus uncomfortably high.

Apart from apprehensions about over-heating of the economy, such unbridled expansion of credit has taken a toll on the quality of credit. RBI has expressed some concern about the recent rapid growth of bank lending to the sensitive sectors, namely, real estate, housing and capital market exposures.

RBI has subsequently tightened credit expansion to these sectors by enhancing provisioning and risk weight. This was also necessary to tackle rapidly escalating asset prices and their possible impact on banks' balance sheets.

Management of Capital Flows

Finally, what is the 'biggest challenge' facing monetary authorities today '...risks to inflation and inflation expectations would continue to demand priority in policy monitoring, with the biggest challenge being the management of capital flows and the attendant implications for liquidity and overall stability, especially in the context of the rapid escalation in asset prices driven by capital flows' (Reddy, 2008). The RBI would therefore continue with its policy of active demand management of liquidity through appropriate use of the credit reserve ratio (CRR) stipulations, open market operations (OMO) including the new market stabilisation scheme (MSS) and liquidity adjustment facility (LAF). The MSS introduced in April 2004 has emerged as the most powerful instrument for liquidity sterilisation: security issuances under the scheme do not provide budgetary support and interest costs are borne by the Government. The ceiling on the outstanding amount under the scheme for the year 2007-08 was successively raised on four occasions to Rs. 2,50,000 crore. The actual outstanding amount was Rs. 1,70,670 crore on 1st February 2008.

In a similar vein CRR was raised by 250 basis points since December 2006.

Changes in fixed reverse repo/repo rates set by RBI from time to time for the conduct of LAF, under which it conducts daily auctions for banks have emerged as the main instrument for interest rate signalling in the Indian economy.

Fiscal Prudence

In the history of Indian public finance, harmonising fiscal policy with monetary policy has always posed a problem. Many RBI Governors were haunted by the spectre of mounting budget deficit. The post-reforms period is notable for a great leap forward towards fiscal prudence. A beginning in this direction was made in April 1997 with the delinking of budget deficit from its automatic monetisation through ad hoc Treasury Bills. The Fiscal Responsibility and Budget Management Act, 2003 further strengthened the RBI position by prohibiting RBI from participating in primary issuance of all government securities. RBI withdrew from participating in the primary issues of Central government with effect from April 2006. While on this subject, it may also be added that a greater degree of flexibility has been imparted to monetary management by the more recent removal of statutory floor or ceiling on the level of cash reserve ratio (CRR), and also the removal of the statutory floor of 25 per cent on SLR (statutory liquidity ratio). The effect of these fiscal measures is clearly reflected in the decline in fiscal and revenue deficits. The fiscal deficit of the Centre as a proportion of GDP declined from 5.9 per cent in 2002-03 to 3.4 per cent in

2006-07 and further to 3.2 per cent in 2007-08. Similarly, the revenue deficit declined from 4.4 per cent in 2002-03 to 1.9 per cent in 2006-07 and further to 1.5 per cent in 2007-08. Thus, though the target of zero revenue deficit stipulated in the FRBM Act has not been attained, the fiscal deficit is well around the stipulated target of 3 per cent of GDP.

Concluding Comment

While conceding RBI's contention that management of capital flows is the 'biggest challenge', I would like to add that an equally formidable task is the transifiguration of the banking system or the financial system generally in such a way that it best subserves the promotion of inclusive growth in the real sector. All those involved in the development of the Indian economy—banks including RRBs, cooperatives, microfinance institutions (MFIs), development finance institutions—will have to rethink their own strategies in response to the new emphasis being given on inclusive growth, or broad-based and decentralised growth. New institutional arrangements may have to be forged like bank-SHG linkages, or MFIs-bank linkages. Facilitating inclusive growth is a far more complicated process involving micro planning, evolving area specific solutions, and encouraging participation of a number of actors, including Panchayati Raj Institutions (PRIs), NGOs, SHGs (Mujumdar, 2007). One hopes that RBI will work out a blueprint of such area-specific plans to facilitate participation of banking and financial institutions in this process and also evolve a more equitable interest rate structure.

References

Government of India (2007). *Report on the Conditions of Work and Promotion of Livelihoods in the Unorganised Sector*. p. 221.

Johnson, Simon (2007). "The (Food) Price of Success", *Finance and Development*, Washington, D.C.: IMF. December.

Mboweni, T.T. (2007). "Monetary Policy Challenges in Turbulent Times", 13th Chintaman Deshmukh Memorial Lecture. November 2.

Mujumdar, N.A. (2007). *Inclusive Growth: Development Perspectives in Indian Economy*. New Delhi: Academic Foundation.

———. (2006). "Centrality of Agriculture to India's Economic Development", *Economic and Political Weekly*. January 7.

———. (2005). *Risk Philosophy: An Enquiry into Risks and Uncertainties in Agriculture and the Role of Credit*. NABARD.

———. (ed.) (2002). *Financial Sector Reforms and India's Economic Development*. New Delhi: Academic Foundation.

Rangarajan, C. (2008). *Report of the Committee on Financial Inclusion*. January.

Reddy, Y.V. (2008). "Third Quarter Review of the Annual Statement on Monetary Policy for the Year 2007-08", January 29. p. 49.

———. (2007a). "Evolving Role of the Reserve Bank of India: Recent Developments", Speech delivered on the Foundation Day of the Institute of Development Studies, Jaipur. June 30.

———. (2007b). "Monetary Policy Developments in India: An Overview", Address at the Sveriges Riks Bank, Stockholm, Sweden. September 7.

———. (2007c). "Mid-term Review of the Annual Policy Statement for the year 2007-09", October 30. p. 56.

This is the edited version of the lecture delivered at the Seminar organised in memory of Dr. Manu Shroff by the Gujarat Economic Association, Baroda, February 16, 2008.

14 Transformation of the Banking System

It may be recalled that the Reserve Bank of India (RBI) introduced theme based reports on Currency and Finance since 1998-99. The report for 2005-06[1] belongs to this genre and addresses the issue of financial market development. This 322-page report is a highly analytical document which covers, money, credit and foreign exchange markets, government securities market, corporate debt and equity markets and the whole range of issues relating to financial market integration.

Historically, financial systems in emerging market and developing economies have been dominated by their banking systems. This is also true of India. This pattern has remained more or less unaltered over the years. Households invest only a small portion of their savings in the securities market directly or indirectly through mutual funds. There is a need therefore to 'develop a diversified financial system over a period of time in which both financial institutions and financial markets play important roles' (RBI, 2006: 5). What are the basic objectives of financial market development? To aid economic growth and development. The primary role of financial markets is to intermediate resources from savers to investors, and allocate them in an efficient manner among competing uses in the economy, thereby contributing to growth, both through increased investment and through enhanced efficiency in resource use.

While this broader theme is interesting in itself, what is more exciting is the story, that the Report unfolds, of the transformation of the Indian banking system through reforms from a highly regulated system to a dynamic system which responds to the market signals. No banker can afford to miss this fascinating story. This chapter seeks to sum up four issues: (i) deregulation and liberalisation of the banking system, (ii)

1. RBI (2006).

runaway expansion of credit, (iii) credit penetration, and (iv) inequitable interest rate structure.

Deregulation and Liberalisation of Banking System

Before the early 1990s, banks operated under a regulatory framework characterised by barriers to entry, administered interest rates, pre-emption of resources through high statutory liquidity ratio (SLR) and cash reserve ratio (CRR) and allocation of resources through mechanisms such as maximum permissible bank finance (MPBF) and selective credit controls. Banks suffered from several inefficiencies such as high intermediation cost, low profitability and high non-performing assets (NPAs). It is against this background, that banking sector reforms were initiated in the early 1990s in a phased manner to move away from a financially repressed regime to a liberalised regime through measures such as deregulation of interest rates, entry of new private sector banks, enhanced presence of foreign banks, reduction in statutory pre-emption, introduction of prudential norms, and permitting banks to raise capital from the market. These measures subjected banks to market discipline, enhanced competition and provided productivity and efficiency gains. This is reflected in the intermediation cost (operating expenses as a percentage to total assets) which decelerated from 2.77 per cent in 1996 to 2.11 in 2006 (RBI, 2006: 155). Gross NPAs of scheduled commercial banks as a per cent of gross advances to all sectors declined from 11.4 in 2001 to 3.3 in 2006 (Ibid.: 140).

With a view to enhancing efficiency and productivity through competition, guidelines were laid down for establishment of new banks in the private sector. Since 1993, 12 new private sector banks have been set up. Foreign banks have been allowed more liberal entry. Foreign direct investment in the private sector banks is now allowed up to 74 per cent. Further, the banking sector is undergoing a phase of consolidation. These were 12 mergers/amalgamations since 1999. One hundred and thirty seven regional rural banks (RRBs) were amalgamated to form 43 new RRBs bringing down the total number to 102 from 196 in March 2005. Two major development finance institutions (DFIs), namely ICICI and IDBI were converted into banks, and there was weeding out of unsound non-banking financial companies (NBFCs). There has thus been structural transformation of the banking system.

Runaway Expansion of Credit

Another interesting feature of commercial banking operations is the runaway expansion of bank credit: during the three years 2004-05 to 2006-2007, bank credit expanded by a phenomenal annual average rate of 30 per cent. Is this a 'robust growth', as the Report puts it, or is it a worrying development? Let us look at the factors underlying the acceleration of credit. The major factors responsible for this explosion in credit were: pick-up in economic growth, improvement in the asset quality of the credit institutions, decline in interest rates and rising incomes of households (RBI, 2006: 131). As a result of various measures taken by the Government and RBI, credit flow to agriculture doubled from the annual growth rate of 10.6 per cent during the period 1990-91 to 1999-2000 to 22.2 per cent during the period 2000-01 to 2004-05.

The other two sectors which witnessed rapid growth in credit were households or personal loans and housing loans. Household personal loans registered, on an average, a rise of 38.2 per cent during the five-year period at end-March 2005, as compared to the expansion of 25.2 per cent in the 1990s. The share of personal loans in total bank credit increased from 9.4 per cent at end-March 1990 to 25.2 per cent at end-March 2006.

This rapid expansion is attributed to the fact that restrictions on personal loans were removed and banks were given freedom to decide the quantum, rate of interests, margin requirements and repayment period. These relaxations has had a positive impact on the expansion of personal loans, as reflected in the sharp rise in the number of personal loan accounts.

Within personal loans, housing loans accounted for over one-half of the total loans. Housing loans grew at an average annual rate of 47.7 per cent during the five-year period 2000-01 to 2004-05. The average housing loan amount increased four times between 2000 and 2005. The share of housing loans increased from 2.7 to total loans of banks in 1991 to 11 per cent in 2005.

Robust economic growth has increased the demand for credit. The average annual growth in GDP in the last four years was over 8 per cent: in fact the growth was 9 per cent in 2005-06 and 9.2 per cent in 2006-07. Banks were able to sustain such a high growth in credit by unwinding surplus investment in SLR securities. Now the banks SLR investments have reached the statutory minimum level of 25 per cent, the scope for financing faster growth in credit in future years is limited.

What should be the policy response to such rapid credit expansion? The dominant view seems to be that a generalised policy of tightening credit may prove counterproductive. The appropriate policy response would be to strengthen the financial system by adopting suitable prudential and supervisory norms. The risks involved are not significant because the aggregate ratio of credit to GDP is still moderate, capital adequacy ratios are sufficiently high and NPA ratios are low. 'Nevertheless, keeping in view the risks arising out of rapid credit growth, the Reserve Bank initiated several prudential and monetary measures to slow down the flow of credit to the sensitive sectors and maintain asset quality of banking institutions. The need for banks is to strengthen credit appraisal and post disbursal monitoring' (RBI, 2006: 161).

Credit Penetration

Another related subject on which there is considerable discussion in the Report is credit penetration. Although India has a well-diversified financial system with a wide variety of credit institutions, credit penetration continues to be relatively low in comparison with several developed and emerging economies. For instance, the number of loan accounts per 100 persons in India is 15.8, as compared to 41.8 in Chile, 77.6 in Greece, 32.9 in Malaysia and 24.8 in Thailand (Ibid.: 153). Perhaps the rapid expansion of credit discussed earlier, may reflect to an extent increasing financial deepening. The *All-India Debt and Investment Survey 2002* revealed that the share of institutional agencies in outstanding cash debts of households declined from 66.3 per cent in 1991 to 57.1 in 2002. Concerns about inadequate access to institutional credit in rural areas continue to remain. RBI has taken several measures to extend the outreach of credit institutions in underserved areas. Recently, banks have been permitted to use the services of business facilitators and business correspondents to extend their outreach. 'Banks are now increasingly roping in non-government organisations, SHGs and MFIs to act as intermediaries' (RBI, 2006: 157). The SHG-bank linkage programme is expected to gain further momentum with NABARD taking up a programme for intensification of these activities in 13 identified states, which account for 70 per cent of the rural poor population. The recent emphasis of RBI on 'financial inclusion' has to be interpreted against this background.

One of the major reasons for low credit penetration is lack of awareness of facilities. The underprivileged sections of the society with low levels of income generally hesitate to visit the banks. There is, therefore, need to devise some mechanisms to impart financial education, especially in rural areas. The focus of education should be on educating the general public about the benefits of using formal credit institutions for their requirements.

Inequitable Interest Rate Structure

The Report provides valuable analytical insights into the structure of interest rates, which has been evolved during the low interest rate regime. It was in April 2003 that the system of prime lending rate (PLR) was replaced by a system of benchmark prime lending rate (BPLR). However, the bulk of bank lending has been taking place at sub-BPLR rates: for instance, the share of sub-BPLR lending increased to 82 per cent by March 2007. While higher credit-rated corporates are getting credit at Sub-BPLR rates, agriculture and SSI sectors and other borrowers are generally charged BPLR or in some cases above BPLR rates. The administered interest rate is applicable only in the case of agricultural loans below Rs. 2 lakh, and short-term production credit up to Rs. 3 lakh, and export credit. According to the data of the *All-India Debt and Investment Survey 2002*, about 82 per cent of the rural debt was in the interest range of 12 to 20 per cent, while PLRs of banks were in the region of 11 to 12 per cent. This raises several fundamental questions: 'to compensate for sub-BPLR lending, other segments are charged higher rates of interest, thus leading to cross subsidisation of the economically well-off borrowers by the economically poor borrowers'. (Ibid.: 159). Though the RBI has been advising bank to evolve their own BPLR by taking into account the cost of funds, transaction cost, cover for riskiness, fixation of BPLR continues to be arbitrary rather than rule based. There is therefore the need to take a fresh look at the concept of BPLR with a view to making the interest rate structure transparent and equitable. This is an aspect of banking which is bound to receive greater attention of RBI in the near future, because of its critical importance to efforts towards financial inclusion.

References

RBI (2006). *Report on Currency and Finance, 2005-06: Development of Financial Markets and Role of the Central Bank*. Mumbai.

15 Credit Policy: January 2007

The Spectre of Inflation

The Governor of the Reserve Bank of India (RBI) Dr. Y.V. Reddy released a report on monetary policy on January 31, 2007.[1] A high GDP growth of more than 8 per cent and the runaway expansion of bank credit of say 30 per cent, for three successive years is a formidable combination for any monetary authority to be confronted with. Monetary expansion is well beyond the budgeted parameters. Is the Indian economy overheated? Is the spectre of inflation haunting the Indian economic scenario? It is to the credit of Governor Dr. Reddy that, addressing this situation, he has devised a policy package which seeks to rein in inflation without hampering high GDP growth. Although taken individually these measures appear to constitute a small anti-inflationary dose, collectively, they send a message loud and clear: the phase of soft interest regime is over.

The Macroeconomic Background

Let us begin with the assessment of macroeconomic situation. First, the obsessive concern of RBI for the emerging inflationary pressures is writ large on the 51-page statement of the Governor. Headline inflation has been hardening and has moved well beyond the RBI target of containing inflation within 5 to 5.5 per cent on five occasions during the financial year so far: during the weeks ending October 21, December 30, 2006, and January 6, January 13 and January 20, 2007. On January 20, inflation touched 6.11 per cent. It is this which seems to have triggered the alarm bell and hence containment of inflation forms, the central theme of Governor's statement. 'These spikes of inflation have been contributed to by base effects, supply-side constraints and demand pressures. Overall, the impact of these developments on inflation perceptions due to rise in prices

1. Reddy (2007).

of food articles and inflation expectations, in general, warrant a determined policy response by all concerned to quell such adverse developments for several critical reasons' (Reddy, 2007: 34).

Second, the runaway expansion of bank credit. The high expansion phase which began in 2004 appears to be continuing. On a year-on-year basis non-food credit expanded by 31 per cent on January 5, 2007, on top of an increase of a similar order a year ago. In fact, the incremental credit-deposit ratio of scheduled commercial banks hovered around 100 per cent for most of the months since October 2004. It has witnessed some moderation only in recent months: as on January 5, 2007 the ratio was around 93 per cent—not exactly a healthy trend. Banks have been financing much of the incremental credit expansion by unwinding their surplus investments in Government securities. For instance, banks' holdings of Government and other approved securities (SLR securities) declined to 28.6 per cent of their net demand and time liabilities (NDTL) on January 5, 2007, from the level of 32.6 per cent a year ago. Since the minimum level of statutory liquidity ratio (SLR) is 25 per cent, the cushion available to banks to sustain such a runaway expansion of credit is no longer available to them in future.

In retrospect, one could argue that since GDP growth has accelerated to more than 8 per cent during the last three years—in fact GDP growth in 2005-06 has been now revised upwards to 9 per cent—such expansion in credit was perhaps warranted. But it would be dangerous to permit such unbridled expansion in the coming years. Hence, as Reddy (2007: 31) puts it: 'the policy challenge is to manage the transition to a higher growth path while containing inflationary pressures...' (p. 31).

Third, one byproduct of such unbridled expansion in credit is flow of disproportionately high credit to sensitive sectors; and Reddy has identified such sensitive sectors. 'The continued high growth in the real estate sector, outstanding credit card receivables, loans and advances qualifying as capital market exposures and personal loans is a matter of concern.' (Ibid.: 45). It is important to recognise the link between accelerating inflation and escalating asset prices.

Fourth, money supply has also been growing beyond the planned parameters. On a year-on-year basis, the growth in money supply (M3) at

20.4 per cent on January 5, 2007 was higher than 16 per cent a year ago and well above the projected trajectory of 15 per cent budgeted for 2006-07. Reddy therefore concludes: 'First, early warning signals emanating from rising inflation in an environment of high money and credit growth indicate that monetary policy is still accommodative warranting a policy response' (2007: 38).

Moral Compulsion

Dr. Reddy has added a new dimension to the question as to why there is an imperative need to rein in inflation. High GDP growth is supposed to benefit all but the benefits to the poor accrue with a considerable time lag. In contrast, the impact of high prices is immediate, without any time lag. Again, only about 10 per cent of the working population which is in the organised sector has some sort of inflation hedge, the rest remains unprotected from inflation. In this context the adverse impact of inflation on the poor would be particularly severe if the prices of basic necessities of life rise, as they are doing now. 'Hence, a determined and co-ordinated effort by all to contain inflation without unduly impacting the growth momentum is not only an economic necessity but also a moral compulsion. To the extent the current inflationary pressures are attributable to monetary conditions, it is essential to undertake appropriate measures....' (Ibid.: 42).

Important Measures

These recent trends in the economy, discussed above, that is the combination of high growth and firming inflation coupled with escalating asset prices have complicated the conduct of monetary policy. The enduring strength of capital inflows adds another complicating factor. If we raise interest rates with the objective of containing demand pressures this may act as an incentive to larger inflows of capital. Against this background RBI has adopted a three-pronged approach to contain inflation. First, what RBI has called a 'measured increase in interest rates' to assuage demand pressures. Second, the persistently high credit growth to certain sensitive sectors, discussed above, has the potential for erosion in the quality of credit. Housing is a case in point. Balance sheets of banks need to be fortified against the build-up of loan delinquencies by precautionary provisioning and by enhancement of risk weights assigned to advances to specific sectors. Third, capital inflows are likely to be sustained in future years with their expansionary impact on inflationary pressures. More specifically non-resident deposits have recorded a sizeable increase during this year in response to interest rate differentials. It is necessary to modulate these inflows appropriately. This study provides the rationale for the monetary measures announced on January 31, 2007.

1) Repo Rate

The fixed repo rate has been increased by 25 basis points to 7.50 per cent with effect from 31st January 2007. This means that the cost to banks of borrowing from RBI would rise and obviously banks would try to pass on this cost to borrowers through higher loan rates.

2) Provisioning Requirements

The provisioning requirements in respect of the standard assets in the following four categories of loans and advances (excluding residential housing loans) have been raised to two per cent from the existing level of one per cent: credit to the real estate sector, outstanding credit card receivables, loans and advances qualifying as capital market exposure, and personal loans. The provisioning requirement in respect of residential housing loans remains unchanged at 0.4 per cent for loans up to Rs. 20 lakh and at one per cent for loans above Rs. 20 lakh.

Some changes in provisioning requirements have also been introduced in respect of exposure to non-banking financial companies (NBFCs). This should impart some credit discipline to lending to these sectors.

3) NRI Deposits

The year 2006-07 has witnessed a sizeable increase in non-resident (External) rupee account (NR(E)RA) and foreign currency non-resident (Banks) (FCNR(B)) deposits. Simultaneously, a large growth in advances granted against such deposits is recorded. This phenomenon creates additional complications for conduct of monetary policy. In the present context when India's foreign exchange reserves are quite comfortable there is no reason to provide incentives to attract such deposits. Hence RBI has lowered the interest rate ceilings on NR(E)RA and FCNR(B) deposits by 50 basis points and 25 basis points respectively.

This takes care of one aspect of these deposits. By borrowing against these deposits, the possibility of putting upward pressure on asset prices in sensitive sectors, cannot be ruled out. Banks are therefore henceforward prohibited from granting fresh loans in excess of Rs. 20 lakh against these deposits, either to depositors or to third parties.

Taken individually these measures may constitute a small dose of anti-inflationary medicine but collectively they send a strong message: the soft interest rate regime is over! Already some banks like the ICICI Bank have responded to these measures by raising their lending rates; others are perhaps waiting to follow. The corporate sector in particular will have to rework its strategies to cope with the emerging high interest rate regime.

References

Reddy, Y.V. (2007). *Third Quarter Review of Annual Statement on Monetary Policy for the Year 2000-07*. Mumbai, 31 January.

16 State of Banking: 2006-07

The 'Reports on Trend and Progress of Banking in India', prepared by Reserve Bank of India (RBI) annually have always been authentic documents on the state of banking and the Report for 2006-07 is no exception. This is a highly analytical document covering not only commercial banks, but also cooperative banks, microfinance, non-banking financial companies (NBFCs) and the discourse on financial stability. This brief chapter seeks to focus on the following five aspects of commercial banks: profile of credit, deposits growth, financial performance, financial inclusion, and migration to Basel II norms.

The operations of scheduled commercial banks (SCBs) were marked by a large expansion of credit for the third year in succession. While credit to the retail sector, particularly housing and commercial real estate slowed down significantly, there was a marked improvement in credit flow to the small scale industries (SSI) sector. Deposits growth accelerated. Net profits of SCBs increased sharply mainly due to a jump in net interest income stemming from the increase in the volume of credit.

Profile of Credit

Loans and advances of SCBs continued to register a high growth of 30.6 per cent in 2006-07: this was close on the heels of equally sharp rises of 33.2 per cent and 31.8 per cent in 2004-05 and 2005-06, respectively. Thus for the third year in succession, credit expansion was phenomenal. This runaway expansion in credit has to be contextualised. First, robust macroeconomic performance continued to underpin the performance of banks. National income or gross domestic product (GDP) accelerated to 9.4 per cent in 2006-07 from 9 per cent in the previous year. Real GDP growth during the Tenth Plan period (2002-03 to 2006-07) averaged 7.6 per cent—the highest average rate of growth during any Plan period so far. Second, banks could sustain such an unprecedented growth in credit because they had built up liquidity in the form of excess investments in statutory liquidity ratio (SLR) securities. By bringing down their surplus resources banks have been able to sustain such a phenomenal expansion in credit. This is clear from the fact that incremental credit-deposit ratio was as high as 110 per cent at end-March 2006; and this ratio declined to 81 per cent at end March 2007. This is a welcome sign of some moderation in the run-away expansion of credit.

Although the performance of banks in priority sector lending has improved in recent years, there are sizeable variations in respect of various bank groups. Only five public sector banks achieved the overall target of lending to priority sector and sub-targets of lending to agriculture and weaker sections. Thirty-one banks—12 public sector banks and 19 private sector banks, achieved the overall target, but did not achieve the sub-targets. Ten banks—6 public sector banks and 4 private sector banks—did not achieve the overall target as also the sub-targets.

In retail credit, the growth of retail portfolio of banks decelerated from 40.9 per cent in 2005-06 to 29.9 per cent in 2006-07. Within the retail sub-sector, credit for consumer durables recorded the highest growth at 63.3 per cent in contrast to the previous year's growth of only 17.3 per cent.

It may be recalled that RBI had expressed some concern about the recent rapid growth of bank lending to sensitive sectors, namely, capital markets, real estate and commodities. Credit to these sectors decelerated sharply during 2006-07 from the rise of 74.4 per cent witnessed in 2005-06 to 41.2 per cent. While credit to real estate market decelerated sharply, credit for commodities increased substantially.

Deposits Growth

A distinguishing feature of banking developments in 2006-07 was the quantum jump in deposits growth. Aggregate deposits grew by 24.6 per cent in contrast to a growth of only 17.8 per cent during the previous year. Accelerated growth in term deposits contributed to this impressive performance. Three factors responsible for this phenomenon may be listed. First, there was a clear shift from postal savings to term deposits of banks due to favourable interest rate differentials and there was also the factor of extension of tax benefits to long-term bank deposits. Second, the demand for term deposits increased from the corporate sector entities which were cash-rich: they parked their surplus funds with banks. Third, non-resident deposits registered a growth which was much higher than that during the previous years.

Financial Performance

Operating profits of SCBs increased by 21.2 per cent in 2006-07 compared with an increase of only 6.6 per cent in the previous year. This was the result of higher increase in interest income and a lower increase in operating expenses. Net profits rose by 27 per cent as compared to 17.3 per cent during 2005-06. This improvement in banks balance sheets due to robust financial results led to increased interest in bank stocks. The banking stocks as represented by the Bankex (comprising 18 banking scrips) significantly outperformed the BSE Sensex: while the rise in BSE Sensex was 15.9 per cent in 2006-07, the rise in Bankex was 24.3 per cent.

The asset quality of SCBs improved further during 2006-07. While net non-performing assets (NPAs) to net advances ratio declined to 1 per cent at end-March 2007 from 1.2 per cent a year ago, the ratio of gross NPAs to gross advances fell from 3.3 per cent to 2.5 per cent during the same period.

Financial Inclusion

Financial inclusion refers to delivery of banking services at an affordable cost to the vast sections of disadvantaged and low-income groups who, for a variety of reasons, stand today excluded from the mainstream banking channel. RBI has taken a number of measures in recent years to facilitate faster financial inclusion. In fact 160 districts have been identified for 100 per cent financial inclusion: full coverage has been achieved in the whole of Union Territory of Puducherry and in 28 districts in 8 states. All districts of Himachal Pradesh have also achieved financial inclusion. One hopes that the pace will pick up and it will be possible to cover shortly a large section of the excluded population.

Migration to Basel II Norms

It may be recalled that capital adequacy norms were first introduced, under Basel I framework, in April 1992, when all SCBs were required to maintain a capital to risk-weighted asset ratio (CRAR) of 8 per cent in a phased manner. The stipulated minimum CRAR was raised to 9 per cent from end-March 2000. It may be added that the overall CRAR of all SCBs remained in 2007 at the previous year's level of 12.3 per cent. This means that increase in capital kept pace with the sharp increase in risk-weighted assets, which increased due to the rapid expansion in credit discussed earlier.

The Basel Committee on Banking Supervision (BCBS) released a Revised Framework (RF) in June 2004. In that light RBI issued the guidelines to banks on the new capital adequacy norms (Basel II) on April 27, 2007. The Basel II norms address three types of risks, namely credit risk, market risk and operational risk for minimum capital requirements. The Framework has a three-pillar structure with minimum capital requirements as the first pillar, supervisory review process as the second pillar, and market discipline as the third pillar. While foreign banks operating in India and Indian banks having operational presence outside India are expected to migrate to the Revised Framework with effect from March 2008, all other commercial banks (excluding local area banks and RRBs) are encouraged to migrate to Basel II norms in any case not later than March 31, 2009.

Although banks are required to maintain a minimum CRAR of 9 per cent, on an ongoing basis, RBI may prescribe a higher level of CRAR, to some banks to ensure that the capital held by a bank is commensurate with its overall risk profile.

17 Combating Inflation

Monetary Policy 2007-08

Although the 84-page Annual Policy Statement for the year 2007-08 by Dr. Y.V. Reddy, Governor, Reserve Bank of India, made on April 24, 2007, covers a wide range of substantive issues of monetary policy, the dominant theme remains the containment of inflation.

'While indications of the sustained momentum of growth continued to firm up, inflation in terms of the WPI ruled stubbornly around 6.5 per cent up to March 23, 2007 with this persistence threatening to impact inflation expectations. In terms of consumer prices, inflation was even higher in the range of 7.6–9.8 per cent. Other indicators of demand pressures were also emitting warning signals—money supply 22 per cent; non-food credit growth at 29.5 per cent; capacity constraints; import orders; pricing power of corporates as exemplified in the cement and steel sectors; wage pressures in some sectors; and rising input costs' (pp. 39, 40).

On the eve of the policy announcement, market expectations were that the interest rates would be hiked and as a consequence growth might slow down. Against this background, RBI's decision to maintain the status quo or to keep the key rates—bank rate, repo rate and reverse repo rate, cash reserve ratio (CRR)—unchanged, was good news for the market. The Sensex rose by 208 points or by 1.50 per cent to reach a new high of 14,137. Market welcomed the RBI stance.

In fact there was a touch of irony. Interest rates on home loans 'may become cheaper, *albeit* marginally and only for those customers who have borrowed Rs. 20 lakh or less', predicted Economic Times (25th April, p. 17). This prediction was based on the measure announced by RBI that the risk weight on the residential housing loans to individuals would be reduced from the existing 75 per cent to 50 per cent as a temporary measure. This dispensation will be applicable for loans up to Rs. 20 lakh and will be reviewed after one year... (Governor's Statement, p. 73). Although this was a logical deduction, the general environment is such that no bank has so far announced a reduction of lending rate for this category of borrowers.

In fact RBI has become aggressive in terms of combating inflation. It may be recalled that RBI had articulated, sometime back, a self-imposed medium-term ceiling on inflation at 5 per cent. The Governor's statement has now reframed this medium-term target. 'There are indications supporting the belief that this approach has had a salutary effect on inflation expectations and the socially tolerable rate of inflation has come down. In recognition of India's evolving integration with the global economy and societal preferences in this regard, the resolve, going forward, would be to condition policy and perceptions for inflation in the range of 4–4.5 per cent. This objective would be conducive for maintaining self-accelerating growth over the medium-term' (p. 42). Fighting inflation has thus become the core of monetary policy.

If RBI has chosen not to use the instrument of interest rate to tame inflation, how does it propose to tackle the problem? To answer this question, one has to trace the basic factors which have caused the emergence of inflationary forces, especially the monetary factors. First, the runaway expansion of non-food credit. The Indian economy is on a high growth trajectory, with real GDP recording 9 per cent and 9.2 per cent growth for two successive years 2005-06 and 2006-07. Has this resulted in overheating of the economy? In any case, the acceleration in GDP growth has led to a large expansion in banking and monetary aggregates in 2006-2007. Non-food credit extended by scheduled commercial banks (SCBs) expanded by 28 per cent, close on the heels of a 32 per cent increase recorded during the previous years. It may be noted here that non-food credit expanded by an annual average of 30 per cent during the three years 2003-2006. This meant that the system-level incremental non-food credit-deposit ratio was more than 100 per cent. This ratio was brought down from 109.3 per cent in 2005-06 to 84.6 per cent in 2006-07. The point is that such alarmingly high level of expansion is not sustainable in the medium-term. In a way it was possible to sustain such high growth in credit by drawing down SLR investments. Today this cushion is no longer available because banks' SLR investment are now close to the statutory minimum level. This development would pose challenges to banks in managing liquidity.

Such unbridled expansion of credit has also taken its toll on the quality of credit. The expansion of credit has favoured retail lending, particularly housing, real estate, trade, transport and professional services and non-banking financial companies (NBFCs)—sectors which hitherto were not significant claimants of bank credit. High rates of growth of credit to these segments have given rise to worries about the quality of these assets and the potential non-performance. 'Default rates in regard to Credit Card receivables and personal loans have been rising.' (p. 32).

Another source of financing credit expansion was the unusual buoyancy in deposits growth. Aggregate deposits of SCBs rose by 23 per cent in 2006-07, as against the 18 per cent growth recorded during the previous year. This deposits growth which was the highest growth recorded during the last 11 years, has some distinguishing features. First, there was a clear shift from postal savings to time deposits of banks because bank deposit rates become attractive. Second, the tax incentive available on small savings and equity-linked investments was extended to long-term bank deposits. In fact, there was no reason why bank deposits should have been discriminated against in respect of tax exemptions. The correction of this distortion was indeed welcome and has had the desired impact. Third, banks become aggressive in mobilising deposits to finance their over-extended portfolios.

The impact of such unprecedented credit expansion was reflected in money supply, which remained well above the indicative projections both in 2005-06 and 2006-07. Money Supply (M3) increased by 20.8 per cent in 2006-07 and by 17 per cent in 2005-06. RBI now seeks to contain monetary expansion in 2007-08 at around 17 to 17.5 per cent. Considering that the forecast for GDP growth in 2007-08 is around 8.5 per cent this monetary target should go some way towards containing inflation. The Annual Statement sums up the stance of monetary policy for 2007-08: 'Accordingly, the policy preference for the period ahead is strongly in favour of reinforcing the emphasis on price stability and anchoring inflation expectations' (p. 43). The issue still remains unanswered: if the economy is overheated, because of high GDP growth and injection of large doses of bank credit for three successive years, will deceleration of credit expansion from 28 per cent in 2006-07 to some 25 per cent in 2007-08 be able to cool down the economy?

Towards Full Convertibility

The Annual Policy Statement (2007-08) also includes another important policy component which signifies a step forward towards full convertibility of the rupee. Following the recommendations of the Tarapore Committee on Fuller Capital Account Convertibility (CFCAC), the following three measures have been announced. First, the remittance scheme for individuals has been further liberalised. The present limit of US $50,000 has been raised to US $100,000 per financial year for any permitted current or capital account transaction or a combination of both. Second, for corporates, at present listed Indian companies have a separate limit of 25 per cent of net worth for portfolio investment abroad in listed overseas companies. This limit has now been raised to 35 per cent of net worth. Third, for mutual funds, at present there is an aggregate ceiling on overseas investment of US $3 billion. For providing greater opportunity to mutual funds for investment abroad, this ceiling has now been raised to US $4 billion.

These measures have to be seen in the context of rising foreign exchange reserves of the country, which have now soared to an embarrassingly high level of US $200 billion. These liberalisation measures, one hopes, would lead to optimal utilisation of reserves. While on the subject, we may also mention the recommendation of the 2007 High Powered Expert Committee (HPEC) on Making Mumbai an International Financial Centre (MIFC) (Chairman: Percy Mistry): it advocates a rapid liberalisation of the capital account over the next 18-24 months, latest by the end of calendar year 2008.

18 Monetary Policy

Prioritising Liquidity Management

Monetary management in India has become a far more complex task today than what it was, say, a decade ago. The pressures on monetary expansion are emanating largely from external sector and these have far-reaching implications for not only monetary management but also for exchange rate management. The interconnectedness of the two is posing a dilemma to the central bank. Tackling such a situation therefore warrants a different mix of policy instruments. This is clearly evident from the statement of Dr. Y.V. Reddy, Governor, Reserve Bank of India (RBI), released on July 31, 2007, on the *First Quarter Review of Annual Monetary Policy for the year 2007-08*.

Broader Canvas

The current financial year which witnessed a sizeable increase in capital inflows provides a typical example of external sectors' dominant influence on domestic liquidity. Foreign institutional investors (FIIs) portfolio inflows rose to \$8.4 billion during 2007-08 (up to July 13), in contrast to an outflow of \$2 billion recorded during the corresponding period of 2006-07. Similarly, gross foreign direct investment (FDI) inflows during April 2007 were placed at \$1.6 billion as compared to \$0.7 billion a year ago. Approvals for external commercial borrowings (ECBs) amounted to \$8.7 billion during April-June 2007, as compared to \$4.4 billion in the corresponding period last year. As a result of these larger inflows, foreign exchange reserves recorded an increase of \$22 billion during the current financial year to soar to \$222 billion on July 20, 2007.

In such a scenario, RBI has two options. Either, it goes on buying dollars from the market, thereby adding to domestic liquidity. Or, if it abstains from doing so, adopting a 'do-nothing policy' as some analysts advocate, with the swelling of dollars in the market, the rupee would tend to appreciate further. While this may be beneficial up to a point, unrestricted appreciation of the rupee may damage the economy in the medium-term. The exchange rate of the rupee against the US dollar which was Rs. 43.59 at end-March 2007 declined to Rs. 40.70 at end-June 2007. Overall, during 2007 (April-June) the rupee appreciated by 6.63 per cent against US dollar. The appreciation against pound sterling was 4.41 per cent and against the euro by 5.19 per cent. Already, exporters are bemoaning the erosion of their international competitiveness because of the appreciation of the rupee. In response, Government of India announced, on July 12, 2007, a package of measures to provide some subvention to exporters for a temporary period. The package involves an outlay of Rs. 1,400 crore and includes tax/duty concessions and subsidised export credit.

Growth Prospects for 2007-08

It is against this broader canvas, that the stance of monetary policy for the next three quarter of 2007-08 needs to be assessed. RBI has stuck to its earlier forecast of GDP growth of 8.5 per cent in 2007-08. It may be added here that the Prime Minister's Economic Advisory Council (PMEAC) has set the forecast of growth a little higher as 9 per cent. In any case, monetary policy can never be so fine-tuned and hence a half-a-percentage difference does not matter. In fact the destruction of crops by the recent floods in different parts of the country may bring down agricultural growth and RBI's lower estimate may prove more realistic. Further, reiterating its commitment to contain inflation, RBI sets the inflation target at 5 per cent in 2007-08, emphasising that the medium-term target would continue to remain in the region of 4 to 4.5 per cent—a level which RBI calls as 'the policy tolerance threshold'.

In consonance with the outlook for growth and inflation, the projected expansion in money supply (M3) at 17 to 17.5 per cent remains unchanged from what was envisaged in April 2007.

Stance of Monetary Policy

Perhaps the most important aspect of policy change in emphasis that this *First Quarterly Review* reveals is that RBI will be more aggressive in liquidity management in the ensuing months. 'Keeping the above in view, recent developments in financial markets in India and potential uncertainties in global markets, warrant a higher priority for managing appropriate liquidity conditions in the policy hierarchy at the current juncture' (p. 48). In other words, RBI will pursue an active demand management of liquidity through appropriate use of cash reserve ratio (CRR), open market operations (OMO), market stabilisation scheme (MSS) and liquidity adjustment facility (LAF). Perhaps, what has triggered this change in emphasis is the recent appreciation of the rupee.

The large capital inflows have resulted in the surfeit of liquidity and this had serious adverse repercussions on the money market. The interest rate in the call market declined from an average of 14 per cent in March to 8 per cent in April, to 7 per cent in May and 2 per cent in June 2007. In July 2007, the rate dipped to the lowest level of 0.90 per cent. Such an absurd situation is fraught with dangers of misuse of funds or at least misallocation of funds. This was perhaps the last straw on the back of RBI which provoked RBI to assume an aggressive posture to siphon off excess liquidity.

The Measures

The most important measure announced on July 31, is the raising of the CRR of scheduled banks to 7 per cent, with effect from August 4, 2007, from 6.5 per cent. This would have the effect of reducing the excess liquidity by around Rs. 14,000 crore. It is the sterilisation of liquidity of such magnitude at one go, as it were, which would moderate the overall liquidity. The second important measure relates to the reverse repo facility under which RBI absorbs liquidity at a fixed rate of 6 per cent on a daily basis up to a level of Rs. 3,000 crore. This ceiling of Rs. 3,000 crore has now been removed. In other words RBI will activate this instrument to siphon off larger quantum of resources, if warranted. Further, RBI has hinted that it may choose to conduct repo/reverse repo auctions at a fixed rate or at variable rates, as circumstances warrant.

The focus of monetary policy will thus be on management of liquidity.

How have the commercial banks reacted to the raising of CRR? Many public sector banks (PSBs) led by State Bank of India (SBI) have reduced the deposits rates marginally. This would reduce the cost of funds to banks thus compensating in part for the loss involved in freezing of bank's resources.

The Government of India, on its part, has also made its contribution to liquidity management through tightening of rules governing external commercial borrowings (ECBs). As discussed earlier, ECBs account for sizeable proportion of overall inflow of foreign capital. The Government of India's announcement on August 7 stipulates that companies can raise only up to $20 million abroad for rupee expenditure and only with prior approval of RBI. With the country's robust forex reserves, there are really no compelling reasons why the corporate sector should borrow from abroad on such a massive scale. The new measure should moderate the magnitude of inflow through this source.

19 Credit Policy for 2008-09

The Spectre of Inflation

The announcement of the monetary policy for 2008-09, by the Governor Dr. Y.V. Reddy, Reserve Bank of India (RBI) on April 29, 2008, had attracted more than normal interest such events usually claim. There were at least three reasons for such extraordinary interest. First, the spectre of inflation loomed large on the horizon. Inflation based on the wholesale price index (WPI), on a year-on-year basis stood at 7.4 per cent at end-March 2008, as compared with 5.9 per cent a year ago. As on April 12, 2008 the headline inflation stood at 7.3 per cent as against 6.3 per cent a year ago. Was this a monetary phenomenon? Money supply had risen above indicative projections persistently through 2005-2007 largely due to sizeable accretions to RBI's foreign exchange assets and acceleration of credit and deposit growth, particularly the latter, in 2007-2009. For instance, money supply (M3) rose by 20.7 per cent in 2007-08 close on the heels of an increase of 21.5 per cent in 2006-07. In fact the trend in inflation seems to have persisted in subsequent weeks, with WPI recording a rise of 7.5 per cent on April 19. This level of inflation, which is the highest during the last 42 months, is far above the tolerance limit of 5 per cent and hence reining in of inflation had acquired a sense of urgency. Second, the global environment for control of inflation has turned hostile. Prices of crude oil which have rebounded since July 2007, recorded a rise by 83 per cent upto April 25, 2008 from their level a year ago, with the price soaring to a record level of around US $120 per barrel. In the global food grains market, prices of major crops wheat, corn and soyabeans had risen by 56 per cent, 58 per cent and 86 per cent respectively, from a year ago, in response to surge in demand. The outlook for global growth has worsened. World gross domestic product (GDP) growth in real terms, on the basis of market exchange rates, is expected to decelerate from 3.7 per cent in 2007 to 2.6 per cent in 2008 and 2009. Third, Governor or RBI seemed to be in a mighty hurry to tackle inflation. Although the policy announcement was scheduled on April 29, the Governor thought it appropriate to announce on April 17, the raising of the cash reserve ratio (CRR) of banks by 50 basis points to 8 per cent. This was required to be implemented in two phases, to 7.75 per cent from April 26, and to 8 per cent from May 10, 2008. With this increase in CRR, an amount of Rs.18,500 crore of resources of banks would be impounded.

Did this pre-empting in a way, of the policy pronouncement of April 29, symbolise the pressing of the panic button by Governor, RBI? This gave rise to apprehensions, on the part of the private sector, that the monetary policy package would be tough, probably with raising of interest rates and tightening of credit. Would the April 29 measures reflect a trade-off between growth and inflation?

Measures: April 29

Against this build-up of inflation spectre, the announcement of monetary measures on April 29 came as an anti-climax. The bank rate was kept unchanged at 6 per cent, so also the repo and the reverse repo rates at 7.75 per cent and 6 per cent respectively.

The only change announced was further raising of CRR by 25 basis points to 8.25 per cent with effect from May 24, 2008. This would mean a further impounding of banks' resources by another Rs.9,000 crore or so.

This was a master stroke by the Governor who proved that the apprehensions of the private sector that the interest rate structure would be adjusted upwards were misplaced. Subsequently many banks have clarified that lending rates would not be raised. This also demonstrated that RBI was as much concerned with growth as with control of inflation.

The Rationale

The Governor's 79-page policy statement provides analytical insights into the phenomenon: the battle against inflation is far from over; but the manner in which it needs to be tackled would be different somewhat because the current inflation is not a purely monetary phenomenon. The Governor's statement also makes it clear that in the measures taken there is no trade-off between growth and inflation. In fact, RBI places GDP growth in 2008-09 in real terms, in the range of 8 to 8.5 per cent. Although there is some deceleration in growth from 8.7 per cent in 2007-08 to 8 per cent, what is important is that the Indian economy continues to be in the high growth league.

The stance of monetary policy for 2008-09 has been spelt out as follows: 'the policy endeavour would be to bring down inflation from the current high level of above 7 per cent to around 5.5 per cent in 2008-09 with a preference for bringing it close to 5 per cent as soon as possible, recognising the evolving complexities in globally transmitted inflation. The resolve, going forward, would continue to be to condition policy and perceptions for inflation in the range of 4-4.5 per cent so that an inflation rate of around 3 per cent becomes a medium-term objective consistent with India's broader integration into the global economy and with the goal of maintaining self-accelerating growth over the medium-term' (Para 87, page 37).

To the extent that monetary factors are responsible for inflation, RBI seeks to moderate money supply. 'In view of the resulting monetary overhand, it is necessary to moderate monetary expansion and plan for a rate of money supply in the range of 16.5-17 per cent in 2008-09 in consonance with the outlook on growth and inflation so as to ensure macroeconomic and financial stability in the period ahead' (Para 88, page 37).

Supply-Side Pressures

The most important analytical insight provided by the Dr. Reddy is that the pick-up in inflation during the fourth quarter of 2007-08 has mainly emanated from supply-side pressures: these include the one-off increase in domestic petrol and diesel prices to partially offset the global crude oil price rise over the year; rising prices of wheat and oilseeds; and the adjustment in steel prices in March 2008 due to surge in international prices. Several administrative measures have been taken to moderate the price rise: these include reducing import duty on rice and edible oils, ban on exports of non-*basmati* rice and pulses, increase in the minimum export price relating to *basmati* rice. Stock limits on selected agricultural commodities have been imposed. The April 29 monetary policy package also includes a directive that banks should ensure that bank finance is not used for hoarding of commodities (page 64).

The market responded positively to the cumulative impact of credit policy of RBI and the administrative measures taken by Government. The Sensex rose by 363 points on April 29.

In fact, in India the crux of containing inflation lies in controlling prices of essential commodities or primary articles which have a weightage of 22 per cent in WPI basket. And in this area the prospects are quite bright. Total food grains production is expected to reach in 2007-08 to an all-time high of 227.3 million tonnes from 217.3 million tonnes in 2006-2007.

The impact of this bumper harvest is reflected in level of current procurement of wheat and rice. Food Corporation of India (FCI) has already exceeded its procurement target of 150 lakh tonnes of wheat. By the end of the season, its total procurement may reach around 170 lakh tonnes. Similarly, FCI is also confident of exceeding its target of 27 million tonnes of rice by the end of the rice marketing season which ends in October. This more than comfortable supply position should have a salutary impact on prices of not only these two major cereals but on food articles in general.

This optimistic outlook is further reinforced by the forecasts of monsoons which predict a near-normal rainfall at 99 per cent of the long period average for the country as a whole in the 2008 southwest monsoon season. Irrespective of what happens to global availability of rice and wheat and to their global prices, India can enjoy the luxury of isolating itself from these forces.

Thus in the India-specific situation of today, the food grains position and outlook would substantially reduce the burden of monetary policy in its efforts to contain inflation.

Other Developments

The policy statement also provides information on a number of developments in the financial sector. Three of them may be briefly mentioned here: financial inclusion, microfinance and Report of the Financial Stability Forum.

Financial Inclusion

It may be recalled that 277 districts had been identified for 100 per cent financial inclusion. Out of these, the target has been achieved in 134 districts in 18 states and 5 union territories. Interestingly, all districts of Haryana, Himachal Pradesh, Karnataka, Kerala, Uttarakhand, Puducherry, Daman and Diu, Dadra and Nagar Haveli and Lakshadweep have achieved 100 per cent inclusion.

Microfinance

As is well-known, the SHG-bank linkage programme has emerged as the major microfinance programme in the country and commercial banks, RRBs and cooperative banks are involved in the exercise. There were in all 28.94 lakh SHGs with an outstanding bank loans of Rs.12,366 crore. Commercial banks accounted for 70 per cent of outstanding loans, while RRBs and cooperative banks accounted for 23 per cent and 7 per cent, respectively.

Report of the Financial Stability Forum (FSF)

In the wake of the recent turmoil in the global financial markets, the FSF brought out, in April 2008, a report identifying the causes and weaknesses in the international financial markets. The report embodies proposals for strengthening prudential oversight of capital, liquidity and risk management, enhancing transparency and valuation, changing the role of credit ratings, etc. RBI has already put in place regulatory guidelines covering many of these aspects. The status of RBI's response to these proposals is indicated in the policy statement.

20 Monetary Policy: January 2009

Maintaining the Status Quo?

Amid market expectations, corporate sector lobbying, and persistent pressures from some Government of India policymakers, Dr. D. Subbarao, Governor, Reserve Bank of India (RBI) chose to maintain the status quo in respect of further injection of liquidity and reduction of interest rates. In his *Third Quarter Review of Monetary Policy 2008-09*, announced on January 27, 2009, the Governor kept the bank rate unchanged at 6 per cent; the cash reserve ratio (CRR) was kept unchanged at 5 per cent; the repo rate and the reserve repo rates were kept unchanged at 5.5 per cent and 4 per cent, respectively.

The only change introduced was the extension of the two liquidity support facilities under liquidity adjustment facility (LAF), which were valid upto end-June 2009 to end-September 2009. These facilities were designed to meet funding requirements of mutual funds (MFs), non-banking financial companies (NBFCs) and housing finance companies (HFCs).

In a 37-page highly analytical document, Governor Subbarao has spelt out the rationale for this action. He argues forcefully that we should not be swayed by what other central banks, particularly of developed countries which have been afflicted by the deepening recessions, have done. These central banks may have had their own reasons for injection of massive liquidity and for reducing interest rates to near zero levels. 'While we have certainly studied and evaluated measures taken by other central banks around the world, we have calibrated and designed our responses keeping in view *India's Specific economic context'* (page 31). This is the key statement which forms the basis of the analysis embodied in Governor's policy response.

How is India different from other developed countries suffering from recession? First, the world economic outlook is bleak. According to the IMF, global real GDP growth is expected to decelerate from

2.6 per cent in 2008 to 1.1 per cent in 2009. The US, the UK, the Euro area and Japan which together account for nearly half of the world GDP are already in recession. In contrast, the growth projection for the Indian economy is still high. Admittedly there is some slowing down in industrial activity and weakening of external demand as reflected in the decline in exports. The growth projection has been scaled down from 7.5 to 8 per cent to say, 6.5 to 7 per cent. Thus India continues to be the second fastest growing economy in the world even in 2009-10.

Second, the international financial system continues to remain dysfunctional amid extreme risk aversion, freezing of money and credit markets and disruption of international capital flows. The global financial system which was passing through an unprecedented turmoil since August 2007 experienced a jolt in September 2008 when the failure of Lehman Brothers led to widespread panic. Many systemically important commercial banks, investment banks, insurance companies and other financial institutions in the US and Europe collapsed and quite a number of them had to be bailed out.

The Indian scenario offers a contrast 'Barring some tightness in liquidity during mid-September to early October 2008, the money, foreign exchange and government securities markets have been orderly as reflected in market rates, spreads, and transaction volumes relative to those observed during normal times. India's banking system remains healthy, well-capitalised, resilient and profitable credit markets have been functioning well and banks have been expanding credit, notwithstanding the perceptions in some quarters of lack of adequate credit from banks to the commercial sector' (page 20). In fact, the incremental credit-deposit ratio at 81 per cent on January 2, 2009 was higher than the corresponding ratio of 63 per cent, a year ago.

A number of measures taken by RBI since mid-September 2008, like cumulative reduction in the CRR and unwinding of market stabilisation scheme (MSS), have resulted in the injection of massive liquidity of Rs. 3,88,045 crore (page 29).

Although the January 2009 measures did not reduce any policy interest rates, the Governor's message to banks is unmistakable. 'As a result of several measures initiated by the Reserve Bank since mid-

September 2008, banks' cost of funds would come down. This should encourage banks to reduce their lending rate, in the coming months' (page 16).

What strengthened further the case for reduction in lending rates was the sharp decline in inflation. Headline inflation, as measured by year-on-year variations in the wholesale price index (WPI) declined by more than half from its intra-year peak of 12.9 per cent on August 2, 2008 to 5.6 per cent by January 2, 2009. Although, the fall in international commodity prices has helped the decline in the index, the contribution of effective management of domestic demand cannot be overlooked. In fact the rate of inflation is anticipated to decline further to some 3 per cent by end-March 2009.

Following this exhortation of RBI to banks, the Finance Minister Pranab Mukherjee met public sector banks (PSBs) on February 2 and stated, 'We must support the development of sectors which will immediately boost growth and throw up employment opportunities. In view of the contracting global demand we have to focus on the development of domestic demand by stimulating demand in rural areas and in labour intensive sectors'.

Thus nudged by both RBI and Government, PSBs appear poised to cut lending rates. In fact following RBI's exhortation, the Punjab National Bank (PNB) cut its benchmark lending rate by 50 basis points to 11.5 per cent—the lowest among all banks. Similarly, the State Bank of India (SBI) announced, on February 1, that it would provide housing loans at a rate of 8 per cent to all fresh borrowers. The going rates ranged from 8.5 per cent to 11 per cent depending on the size of the loan. The lead given by PNB and SBI may probably result in easing of lending rates generally by most, if not all, PSBs.

On the whole, a superficial reading of the January 27 monetary and credit policy measures may give an impression that RBI is keen on maintaining the status quo in terms of the interest rate structure. However, the net result has been the easing of the lending rate structure. This was rendered possible because RBI had prepared the ground for reduction of cost of funds to banks.

There is another analytical misapprehension about bank credit which the Governor's statement has clarified. The growth in non-food bank credit as on January 2, 2009 at 24 per cent was higher than the expansion of 22 per cent witnessed a year ago. Despite this, a view is often expressed that there is dearth of credit. This is attributable to the fact that there is shrinkage in the flow of funds from the non-bank sources, notably the capital market and external commercial borrowings: for instance, such flow was around Rs. 1,91,470 crore in 2008-09, (up to January 2) as compared to Rs. 2,74,563 crore during the corresponding period of 2007-08. While bank credit has substituted for the shortfall in other sources of funds, to some extent, it has been unable to fully substitute for it.

To sum up, our response to the global financial crisis is India-specific. '...while policy responses in advanced economies have had to contend with both financial crisis and recession, in India, the policy response has been predominantly driven by the need to arrest moderation in economic growth' (page 35).

To tackle the external sector led slowdown in growth, two stimulus packages were announced on the fiscal front: the first, announced on December 7, 2008 included raising of public expenditure by Rs. 20,000 crore to boost infrastructure development. The second, announced on January 2, 2009 was wide-ranging in scope: enhancing spending power of states, offer of sops to exporters and small-scale sector and raising the level of protection of cement and steel sectors. RBI's massive injection of liquidity in the financial system to facilitate easing of lending rates has to be viewed in the totality of the context of stimulating the economy.

21 Corporate Sector, Interest Rates and Credit Policy

In the run-up to the Annual Credit Policy Announcement scheduled on April 21, 2009, by Reserve Bank of India (RBI) Governor Dr. D. Subbarao, there was a build-up of tremendous pressure on RBI to reduce lending rates. Even the Ministry of Finance and the Planning Commission joined the chorus of the corporate sector. There were at least three reasons for supporting this plea. First, since September 2008 RBI's policy response has been designed to mitigate the adverse impact of the global financial crisis on the Indian economy and low interest regime would be consistent with this objective. Second, headline inflation, as measured by year-on-year variations in the wholesale price index (WPI) declined sharply from the intra-year peak of 12.91 per cent on August 2, 2008 to 0.26 per cent by March 28, 2009. Inflation declined further to 0.18 per cent on April 4. This consistent decline, therefore warrants a downward adjustment of lending rates. Third, the policy measures taken by RBI since mid-September 2008 have resulted in the pumping of massive liquidity of Rs. 4,22,000 crore in the system. In fact, the banking system today is highly liquid with surplus funds of banks of some Rs. 1,16,470 crore parked with RBI, as at end-March 2009.

Policy Measures

While recognising the factors mentioned above, RBI chose to respond in a symbolic manner, rather than a substantive manner. RBI reduced the repo rate by 25 basis points from 5 per cent to 4.75 per cent; and the reverse repo rate by 25 basis points from 3.5 per cent to 3.25 per cent. Both the changes became effective from April 21, 2009.

Both the bank rate (BR) and the cash reserve ratio (CRR) were retained unchanged at 6 per cent and 5 per cent respectively.

With the surfeit of liquidity as mentioned above, and the cost of borrowing by banks from RBI reduced, RBI hoped that banks would reduce their lending rates. In fact, Governor Subbarao was more explicit: 'Notwithstanding the above factors, there is still scope for banks to reduce their lending rates. Pointing to the current WPI inflation rate near zero, some have argued that the real lending rates are very high. The point-to-point variation in WPI exaggerate the level of real interest rate due to divergence between various price indices as also the inflation expectations. Notwithstanding computational challenges, even when inflation is taken as 4.0-4.5 per cent based on the underlying trend, real lending rates would still appear to be high. Banks, therefore, much strive to reduce their lending rates further' (RBI, 2009: 19).

The message was thus loud and clear. In fact, the response of banks to the Governor's exhortation was quick. ICICI Bank reduced its prime lending rate by 50 basis points. Other banks, particularly public sector banks (PSBs) followed. Interest rates on home loans declined and high rated corporates could raise from banks' short-term money, say up to one year at around 6 per cent. The objective of the Governor to ease lending rates seems to have been largely achieved.

Corporate Sector's Perception

The corporate sector has been arguing that the quantum of credit flow to the commercial sector has shrunk and that the lending rates of banks continued to be high, especially when judged by the sharp decline in inflation rate. The Governor of RBI has provided satisfactory answers to both these contentions.

First, regarding the quantum of credit. Admittedly, the expansion in non-food credit in 2008-09 was lower than that of 23 per cent recorded in 2007-08. There were several reasons for this moderation in credit growth. There was slowdown of the economy in general and in the industrial growth in particular. After clocking annual GDP growth of nearly 9 per cent, on an average, over the last five years 2003 to 2008, GDP growth dipped to around 6.5 per cent in 2008-09. Industrial growth during April-February 2008-09 declined to 2.8 per cent from 8.8 per cent in the corresponding period of the previous year. No wonder the demand for bank credit slackened in 2008-09.

Even taking the commercial sector as a whole, the flow of bank credit declined only marginally from Rs. 4,44,807 crore in 2007-08 to Rs. 4,14,902 crore in 2008-09. The flow of resources to commercial sector from sources other than banks—like the capital market, financial institutions etc., recorded a sharp decline from Rs. 335,698 crore in 2007-08 to Rs. 2,64,138 crore in 2008-09. In the context of the sharp decline in GDP discussed above, the argument that the size of resources available to commercial sector was inadequate is not thus sustainable.

Why did RBI not bring about a drastic reduction in, say CRR or in repo rates? The answer lies in the fact that while inflation measured by WPI is at near-zero level, inflation based on consumer price indices (CPIs) continues to be near double–digit level, reflecting mainly a firm trend in prices of food articles. The prices of food articles are still ruling high. The spectre of inflation is yet to be laid to rest.

The Governor's policy statement is quite explicit: 'The analysis of the last four years suggest that WPI inflation and CPI inflation moved, by and large, in tandem till April, 2007. Thereafter inflation measured in WPI and CPI tended to diverge. However, the divergence in the recent period has been unusually high reflecting the volatilities in commodity prices which have higher weight in WPI. With the decline in WPI inflation, CPI inflation is expected to moderate in the coming months. For its overall assessment of inflation outlook for policy purposes, the Reserve Bank continuously monitors the full array of prices indicators' (page 71).

Interest Rate Structure

Financial sector and banking sector reforms implemented in the 1990s have resulted in the emergence of an inequitable interest rate structure, a structure designed to pamper the corporate elite and which is biased against the small borrower generally. The RBI's *Report on Currency and Finance 2005-06* provides valuable insights into the structure of interest rates. The bulk of bank lending has been taking place at sub-BPLR. To quote the RBI Report (2006), 'To compensate for such Sub-BPLR lending other segments are charged higher rates of interest thus leading to cross subsidisation of the economically well-off borrowers by the economically poor borrowers' (page 159). There was a time when a triple-A rated company could raise money from banks at 6 per cent while, a small farmer was required to pay an interest of 12 per cent. Although this has changed, with the small farmer now getting subsidised credit at 7 per cent, the basic issue remains. As the RBI admits, 'Over time however, the system of BPLR has evolved in such a manner that it has lost its relevance as a meaningful reference rate as bulk of loans is advanced below BPLR.' It has also become non-transparent. Hence, the Governor announced the setting up of a Working Group to review the present BPLR system and suggest changes to make credit pricing more transparent. The Group has been asked to submit its Report by end-August 2009.

Outlook for 2009-10

The RBI would continue to endeavour to boost growth especially in the context of the present global crisis. 'The Reserve Bank is committed to providing ample liquidity for all productive activities on a continuous basis.' Hence, RBI projects growth in non-food credit of 20 per cent in 2009-10. This is feasible in the context of the projected parameters of other variables: money supply (M3) growth at 17 per cent and growth of aggregate deposits of scheduled commercial banks at 18 per cent. Inflation as measured by WPI would be around 4 per cent. GDP growth is projected at 6 per cent. With all the advanced economies in a synchronised recession, global GDP is projected to decline in 2009-10 by 0.5 per cent to 1 per cent. In this context, the Indian economy posting a growth of 6 or above 6 per cent for two successive years 2008-09 and 2009-10 is indeed remarkable.

References

RBI (2009). *Annual Policy Statement, 2009-10*. April 21, Mumbai.

22 Inflation Management in India

At the outset, it should be recognised that the phenomenon of inflation as it has manifested today is characterised by certain unique features and the conventional techniques of control of inflation based on the textbook definition of inflation, namely, 'too much money chasing too few goods' may not be the appropriate instruments. It would be simplistic to interpret the current situation in terms of the quantity theory of money or, the money-output-prices formula. Since the current inflation is drought—exacerbated, the conventional prescription of curtailing money supply and/or bank credit may prove counterproductive. An objective analysis of the situation seems to warrant micro management, rather than macro management of inflation.

Nature of Inflation

First, inflation measured by the wholesale price index (WPI) was minus 1.7 per cent for the week ended July 11, 2009. This negative WPI inflation is expected to persist for a few more months. The currently observed negative WPI inflation is a statistical illusion reflecting the high base of the previous year. It should not be interpreted as structural deflation resulting from aggregate demand contraction.

Second, inflation is really reflected in consumer price indices (CPI) which indicate an inflation of around 11 per cent. Essential commodities as a group have recorded a rise of 10-60 per cent between July 11, 2009 and July 2008. It is this price rise which is disturbing and on which policy needs to focus.

Third, in the period subsequent to July 11, 2009, there has been a further rise in prices largely spurred by the poor monsoon. In fact, drought conditions are prevailing in nearly half the total number of districts in the country. The rise is particularly alarming in some sub-groups; for instance in the case of pulses, prices of *tur dal* have soared to more than Rs. 100 per kg. Since pulses are the only source of protein for the lower middle class and the poor, this spurt is disturbing. The inflationary expectations arising from bad monsoon needs to be tackled, by micro management.

Fourth, the fiscal deficit jumped to 6.8 per cent of GDP in 2008-09, from the level of 2.7 per cent in the previous year. Thus, the targets stipulated under the Fiscal Responsibility and Budget Management (FRBM) Rules had to be abandoned. But there is a difference. The fiscal deficit soared not so much because of government consumption as because of the stimulus measures taken by the government. The three fiscal stimulus packages in the form of tax relief to boost demand and increased expenditure on public projects to crate employment and public assets aggregated to Rs. 1,86,000 crore or 3.5 per cent of GDP. The point is that the potential increase in GDP as a result of these packages will offset, to some extent, the inflationary impact of the budgetary deficit.

The moot point is that the conventional instruments of control of inflation through containment of aggregate demand—either through restraint on money supply or on bank credit—are not quite relevant for tackling the current situation.

Vulnerable Sections of Population

The issue boils down to protecting the vulnerable sections of the population from the impact of inflation and hence micro management. Fortunately despite the bad monsoon, the supply side of food grains remains comfortable. For three consecutive years 2005-06 to 2007-08, food grains production recorded an average annual increase of over 10 million tonnes. Hence, we have started the year 2009-10 with comfortable food grains stocks with the Food Corporation of India (FCI) of some 50 million tonnes of rice and wheat. Thus, even if rice production during the current year 2009-10 declines by 10 million tonnes because of bad monsoon, we can meet the normal requirements of consumption.

In India, the food grains market is a segmented market, with the public distribution system (PDS) providing a sort of safety net for the poor. Food grains are distributed at subsidised rates to some 6.5 crore below the poverty line (BPL) families. Offtake of food grains under targeted public distribution system (TPDS) and other welfare schemes has gone up from 31.3 million tonnes in 2002-03 to 37.3 million tonnes in 2007-08. In a drought year, such offtake may increase further and we have enough stocks to meet the demand.

It should be added here that the Maharashtra government is planning to distribute *tur dal* at subsidised rates through PDS. Such policy responses at the micro level are critical to inflation management.

The National Programme of Mid-day Meals in schools covers, since April 2008, all children studying in government, local body and government-aided primary and upper primary schools. During 2008-09, 11.74 crore children benefited from the scheme. Then there is the Integrated Child Development Services (ICDS) scheme to provide supplementary nutrition to mothers and small children.

These and related schemes do insulate the vulnerable sections of the population from the ravages of inflation.

There is a post-script. The proposed National Food Security Act seeks to provide a statutory basis for a framework which assures food security for all. Every family below the poverty line in rural as well as urban areas will be entitled, by law, to 25 kilograms of rice or wheat per month at Rs. 3 per kilogram. In the light of the drought this year, this proposal has to be necessarily deferred.

Access to Food

It is not enough to ensure availability of food grains in the market; it is also necessary to provide economic access to food grains. In a year of drought particularly, employment in the agricultural and allied sectors shrinks and hence provision of employment is critical. It is in this context that the National Rural Employment Guarantee Scheme (NREGA) launched in 2005 assumes significance. The scheme now covers all the districts in the country and about 4.47 crore households have benefited from it. The scheme has emerged as an important means of providing food security to the vulnerable sections of the rural population.

Food Grains Prices in the Open Market

In terms of regulating the food grains prices in the open market, the FCI should play a proactive role. In a situation of drought and a general apprehension of scarcity, private trade in food grains has the temptation to artificially raise prices by hoarding, etc. This is what used to happen when food grains trade was in the hands of private traders and before the establishment of FCI. But we are treating FCI as a glorified godown keeper. In the present situation, it should emerge as a market-maker. For instance, if prices of rice or wheat rise in some pockets of the country, FCI should unload its stocks in the market and bring prices down. In other words, FCI should act as a watchdog of market prices of rice and wheat and the moment prices begin to soar to unreasonable levels, it should bring down the prices by open sales of these commodities. FCI should thus become an effective countervailing power to private trade.

Common Man's Price Index

The current situation has also exposed the infirmities in our price indicators. For instance, the trends in the wholesale price index (WPI), if interpreted mechanistically, are misleading. Even the essential commodities sub-group which has a weight of 17.8 per cent in the WPI, includes a wider range of commodities: rice, wheat, *jowar*, *bajra*, pulses, potatoes, onions, milk, fish-inland, mutton, chillies (dry), tea, coking coal, kerosene, *atta*, sugar, *gur*, salt, hydrogenated *vanaspati*, rape seed and mustard oil, coconut oil, groundnut oil, long cloth/sheeting, *dhotis*, sarees and voiles, household laundry soap and safety matches. A more confusing bundle of commodities cannot be imagined! That is why perhaps the WPI has today become dysfunctional as a policy tool.

Even under the consumer price indices (CPI), we have four categories: (i) industrial workers, (ii) urban non-manual employees, (iii) agricultural labourers, and (iv) rural labourers. The point that is sought to be driven home is that statistical erudition is no substitute for providing a useable tool for policy.

It would be useful to evolve, for policy purposes, a simple consumer index of the common man. This basket could include only the 'bare necessities'—*roti*, *chawal*, *dal* and *subji*. However rough such an index may be, statistically speaking, it would provide the policymakers a tool to ensure that this index moves within a reasonable range, notwithstanding the overall inflation index.

Part IV

Global Financial Crisis and India

23 The Collapse of the US Financial System

The collapse of the American financial system which we are witnessing today is as traumatic as the collapse of the communist Russia in the 1990s. It has all the elements of a Greek tragedy. Lakhs of Americans have become jobless and homeless: jobless because financial giants have crumbled, and homeless because there are several foreclosures, throwing out those who borrowed for housing but could not repay the installments of loans. Nor is this tragedy confined to the US-Europe is already feeling its impact and its ripples are touching the shores of emerging economies like India.

What started as a subprime mortgage crisis in the US around say August 2007, developed into a cyclonic storm swallowing financial giants and creating hovoc in all financial markets. It was a crisis of confidence. More than 7.5 lakh jobs were lost in 2008. In simple terms, housing loans were extended aggressively to borrowers who did not simply have the capacity to repay. The traditional banking prudence was thrown to the wind. It was reckless lending. Many subprime mortgages were 'ninja loans' standing for no income, no job and no assets. The crisis was thus waiting to happen.

There was the biggest surge in mortgage defaults—bigger than ever witnessed during the last three decades—which threatened to bring down the two mortgage giants, Fannie Mae and Freddie Mac. The US government had to take over these two private mortgage giants through the Federal Housing Finance Agency (FHFA). Again, two of the world's and America's top investment bankers Goldman Sachs and Morgan Stanley were taken over. Lehman Brothers filed for bankruptcy. The insurance giant AIG was also on the verge of collapse and hence, had to be taken over by the government.

All these support efforts culminated in the approval by the US lawmakers of a bank bailout package of $700 billion, on October 3, 2008. This is the largest financial bailout in American history.

This subprime turbulence resulted in the spread of global financial contagions and affected Europe also. At the Summit in Paris on October 5, 2008, European leaders—of France, Germany, Britain, Italy and Luxembourg pledged to bail out their own nation's banks instead of evolving a regional rescue package. The French President stated: 'Each government will act according to its own methods and its own means but in a coordinated manner with other European states.'

The collapse of the American financial system has also raised the more fundamental question: How far can we depend upon market forces to run the financial system? This is important to us because most of the contemporary policymakers and reformers of the Indian financial system are soaked in market theology. We can answer this question with the help of the following episode.

Some 18 months ago, the US Treasury Secretary Henry Paulson who is the architect of the US rescue package mentioned above, addressing an audience at the Shanghai Futures Exchange in China, had emphasised that China is losing trillions of dollars in lost economic potential because of its highly controlled and tightly regulated financial market, particularly capital market. 'An open, competitive and liberalized financial market can effectively allocate scarce resources in a manner that promotes stability and prosperity far better than governmental intervention.' A former adviser to China's central bank, Mr. Yu Yongding reacted after the present US crisis as follows: 'The U.S. financial system was regarded as a model, and we tried our best to copy whatever we could. Suddenly we find our teacher is not that excellent!...' If the US, the citadel of market philosophy, had to resort to nationalisation of its financial giants, does it mean that we have to discard unregulated, totally free financial markets? Indian policymakers will have to ponder over the issue. Prof. Robert Shiller of Yale University has suggested in his book *The Subprime Solution* (2008) the setting up of a financial products safety commission, on the lines of a Consumer Production Agency, to supervise the safety characteristics of various financial products.

What is the impact of the US financial crisis on the Indian economy? Since Indian economy is now integrated with the global economy, it cannot remain insulated from this global turmoil. The obvious victim has been the stock market. For instance, the Dow Jones index was trading below 10,000 on October 6, 2008—the lowest level in the last four years. The US rescue package of $700 billion discussed earlier has not succeeded in lifting the market sentiment. Our own sensex was ruling at 11,802, its lowest level during the last two years. This was bound to happen because foreign institutional investors (FIIs) are exiting from our market and instead of large inflows of funds through this channel, we are witnessing large outflows.

Apart from this, there are no other scars on the Indian financial system. Fortunately, India has escaped the catastrophe because of a number of factors. The credit derivatives market in India is still at an infant stage. In fact, former Governor of Reserve Bank of India, Dr. Y.V. Reddy has received wholesome praise for his cautious approach to developing markets for complex structured credit products and regulating banks tightly. As RBI's Annual Report for 2007-08 puts it: 'Financial stability in India has been achieved through perseverance with prudential policies that prevent institutions from excessive risk taking, and financial markets becoming extremely volatile and turbulent.' RBI's pre-emptive regulations in respect of sensitive sectors namely, capital markets, real estate and commodities have also helped financial sector to remain orderly and financial institutions, especially banks, sound.

To suffice the RBI Report asserts: 'The asset quality and soundness parameters of the Indian banking sector have improved significantly in the recent period and are now comparable with global levels.'

24 Global Financial Crisis and How India is Coping with it

The global financial system is in a crisis of unprecedented dimensions. The situation described as the worst since the 1929 Great Depression continues to remain even today unsettled and uncertain. The problems that originated in large-scale defaults in the US subprime mortgage market and associated market for complex credit derivatives in August 2007, spread like conflagration to the financial sector as a whole in the US first, and then to Europe, and finally to the other parts of the world. There have been sharp declines in stock markets across the world, disruptions in international money markets, and all this is fuelling panic among investors. Will this global financial instability weaken global growth and portend the arrival of global recession? Governments and central banks have responded to the crisis with aggressive and unconventional measures to restore calm and confidence to the markets. Moreover, IMF has come to the rescue of some of the worst affected countries like Iceland, Ukraine and Hungary. In fact IMF would create a new short-term lending facility to channel funds quickly to emerging markets to tide over liquidity problems faced during the current crisis.

Though India is outside the epicentre of this crisis, it cannot be immune to these global developments. The Reserve Bank of India (RBI) is proactive and has taken several steps to minimise the adverse impact of the global financial crisis on the Indian economy. Dr. D. Subbarao, Governor, RBI devoted a considerable part of his 'Mid-Term Review of the Annual Policy Statement for the year 2008-2009' made on October 24, 2008, to provide useful insights into this phenomenon and to indicate how India is coping with the crisis.

But first the global scenario. What happened in September 2008 in the US is now history. In early September two large US government-sponsored mortgage banks were put into conservator ship by the government. In mid-

September a major investment bank filed for bankruptcy and two investment banks were permitted by regulators to become commercial banks. On September 25, money markets ground to a halt, and interbank and repo rates rose to almost record levels. The US financial system had virtually collapsed. The US Treasury announced a rescue plan of $700 billion to clear the bad debt overhang. On October 14, 2008 the Board of Governors of the Federal Reserve System, the US Department of Treasury, and the Federal Deposit Insurance Corporation (FDIC) made a joint statement affirming their resolve to protect the US economy, to strengthen public confidence in the financial institutions, and to foster robust functioning of credit markets.

This wave of banking contagion swept through Benelux (Belgium-Netherlands-Luxembourg), Germany, UK, Spain, Ireland and Iceland and this provoked government intervention; in fact some banks were nationalised, ostensibly on a temporary basis. UK has taken steps to recapitalisation of the banking system. The governments of Australia and New Zealand have announced their decision to guarantee bank deposits.

The world has witnessed unprecedented cooperation among major central banks and joint actions to harmonise their policies. These actions focussed on two objectives: to inject massive liquidity in the system and to reduce policy interest rates. On October 13, 2008, Bank of England (BoE), the European Central Bank (ECB), Bank of Japan (BoJ), and Swiss National Bank (SNB) jointly announced measures to improve liquidity. Similarly, BoE, ECB, the Federal Reserve, the Sveriges Riksbank, and SNB reduced their policy rates by 50 basis points on October 8, 2008. This is a concrete evidence, if proof indeed is needed, of the severity of the crisis facing the global financial system.

As a cumulative result of these disturbances, global economic prospects have been dampened by the weakening of the US economy, the wider repercussions of the ongoing financial market crisis and volatility in the energy, food and commodity prices. According to the *World Economic Outlook* of the IMF, global GDP growth is expected to decelerate from 5 per cent in 2007, to 3.9 per cent in 2008, and further to 3 per cent in 2009.

How is India coping up with this global crisis? Dr. Subbarao, makes the following reassuring statement: 'India's financial sector is stable and healthy. All indicators of financial strength such as capital adequacy, ratios of non-performing assets (NPA), and return on assets (ROA) for our commercial banks, which account for 88 per cent of banking assets, are robust. While many banks and quasi-banking financial institutions in advanced countries suffered large losses and needed substantial capital infusion and bail out packages, Indian banks have been affected only peripherally as they do not have direct financial exposure to the US sub-prime assets...The overall capital adequacy ratio of commercial banks in India is 12.7 per cent, well above the regulatory minimum of 9 per cent and the Basel Accord requirement of 8 per cent...Furthermore, the regulatory mandate of keeping 25 per cent of net demand and time liabilities as SLR and 6.5 per cent as CRR provides an inherent strength to Indian banks'.

One of the major problems faced by Indian banks was the unusual tightening of liquidity in recent weeks caused in part by portfolio investment outflows by foreign institutional investors (FIIs). For instance, portfolio investment outflows recorded net outflows of $7.3 billion during the current financial year upto October 10, 2008, in contrast to net inflows of $18.9 billion in the corresponding period of last year. RBI, therefore, took several measures since mid-September 2008 to assuage the liquidity stress: these included cumulative reduction of 250 basis points in CRR with effect from October 11; a special facility of Rs. 20,000 crore to alleviate the liquidity pressures faced by mutual funds; and provision of Rs. 25,000 crore to banks as the first installment of the Agricultural Debt Waiver and Debt Relief Scheme. The total liquidity support extended to banks thus worked out to a massive figure of Rs. 1,85,000 crore. The easing of the liquidity pressures is reflected in the fact that the call money rates which had touched a peak of 19.8 per cent on October 10, eased to normal levels subsequently.

The most obvious victim of the global meltdown was the stock market. In India the bull market phase from 2003 till early 2008 was unprecendented, the Sensex reaching the peak of 20,873 on January 8, 2008. Subsequently, Sensex started sliding but the fall was precipitious in October 2008, partly reflecting the contagion impact of what was happening in New York or London markets and partly as a result of massive outflows of funds through FIIs, discussed above. The Sensex reached 8,701 on October 24—the lowest level during the last 35 months. Although the index rose somewhat subsequently it has remained below the 10,000 level.

RBI acted again on November 1st, by reducing both CRR and SLRC (statutory liquidity ratio) by 1 per cent each. In effect, this measure meant that banks' usable resources were replenished by Rs. 80,000 crore. Dr. S.S. Tarapore, former Deputy Governor RBI, estimates that total liquidity pumped in by RBI through all these measures adds up to a staggering figure of Rs. 300,000 crore. Is there a surfeit of liquidity now? The underlying idea was to create an enabling environment for banks to reduce their lending rates. The private corporate sector was clamouring for a cheap lending rates structure and with a little nudging from Finance Minister, public sector banks, led by the State Bank of India decided to reduce their prime lending rates by 75 basis points with effect from November 10. One hopes that cheaper credit will spur corporate sector growth.

India has thus, coped with the global financial crisis reasonably well. For instance, RBI has revised its GDP forecast for 2008-09 only marginally down from 8 per cent to some 7.5 per cent. There are two other factors which would help India sustain such a high growth in a world threatened by recession. First externally, crude oil prices have shown a dramatic decline from $145 per barrel on July 3, 2008 to around $60 today. Second, domestically, inflation is decelerating; inflation which had reached 12.76 per cent in August, has now declined below 11 per cent. As Dr. Subbarao has emphasised: 'Quite evidently, the upward shift in our growth trajectory has been possible because of higher pace of investment. Investment as a share of GDP, increased from 25 per cent in 2002-03 to 38 per cent in 2007-08. Of this 13 percentage points increase, as much as 10 percentage points was financed domestically through higher household, public sector and corporate savings'. Interestingly enough, inward foreign direct investment (FDI) has continued to remain buoyant during the current year. Thus, India's growth story is still intact and credible.

25 Global Recession and the Indian Economy

> We are all Keynesians now. Even the right in the United States has joined the Keynesian camp with unbridled enthusiasm and on a scale that at one time would have been truly unimaginable
>
> Joseph Stiglitz (*Economic Times*, 22 December, 2008).

Market fundamentalism embodied in neo-liberalism based on the notion that markets are self-correcting, allocate resources efficiently and serve the public interest well—has collapsed. The 'Washington Concensus' in favour of privatisation, liberalisation and independent central banks focussing exclusively on a single-point agenda of controlling inflation, now stands stripped of its sanctimonious robe. We have now realised that unbridled market forces are not self-correcting, regulation of some sort is needed and that the state has a critical role to play in the management of the economy including the financial sector. The 'hands off' regulatory philosophy of Greenspan has cost the US dearly. Prof. Stiglitz in an interview to an Indian TV channel had remarked: 'Our (US) financial system collapsed because we did not have a Dr. Reddy at the helm', the reference is to Dr. Y.V. Reddy, Former Governor, Reserve Bank of India. There cannot be a better tribute to the management of the Indian financial system.

The global financial meltdown has plunged the US and some other major developed countries into a recession. The Organisation for Economic Co-operation and Development (OECD) has confirmed that a 30-nation area has entered recession. The US GDP is forecast to decline by 0.9 per cent in 2009, the Japanese GDP would decline by 0.1 per cent, while the Euro zone output would shrink by 0.5 per cent. This has prompted some Indian experts to go back to Gottfried Haberler standard work on business cycles. This chapter seeks to argue that such panic reaction is a misadventure. The tsunami of recession has swept many major economies but only its ripples have touched the Indian shores. Even during 2007-08,

Indian economy is expected to record a GDP growth of 7 per cent. This no doubt represents deceleration from the average GDP growth rate of 9 per cent recorded during the last three years. But India's growth rate remains the second highest in the world. Even the outlook for growth in 2009-10 is far from disappointing, given the world economic situation. Some forecasts place the growth at 6.5 or 7 per cent.

Thus, the first point to realise is that India is not in the throes of recession, but the Indian economy is going through a process of deceleration induced by the external sector. Exports have tended to decelerate and the inflow of external resources—either as portfolio investment or as foreign direct investment—have tended to decline. For instance, exports declined in October and November 2008. The exports growth for the first half of the fiscal year was 30 per cent, this rate decelerated to 20 per cent, if the period April to November 2008 is considered. Fortunately, the vulnerability of the Indian economy to these two factors is limited. Merchandise exports constitute only about 15 per cent of GDP. This is in sharp contrast to China, for instance, in the case of which exports account for 35 per cent of its GDP. In the case of investment also, the overwhelming predominance of domestic resources is obvious. Investment as a share of GDP, increased from 25 per cent in 2002-03 to 38 per cent in 2007-08. Of this 13 per cent increase, as much as 10 percentage points was financed domestically through household, public sector and corporate savings. Even foreign direct investment (FDI) remained buoyant this year till October. Inflows during April-September 2008 at $17.2 million were significantly higher than the figure of $7.3 million during the corresponding period of 2007. In October 2008, however, the inflows at $1.5 million were lower than the level of $2 million in October 2007. It is difficult to guess whether the declining trend in inflows would persist in the remaining part of the fiscal year 2008-09. Thus India's growth story remains largely intact. The real question is: how to restore the growth trajectory to a higher level of say, 9 per cent. A correct diagnosis of India's current malaise is indeed a necessary condition for evolving appropriate policy responses to global recession.

A second aspect of the present global crisis which has not received adequate attention in current discussions is: has the collapse of the American capitalist model, particularly its financial model, any implications for India's reforms? This is particularly relevant for financial sector reforms, the blueprint for which has been provided by the Raghuram Rajan Committee (2008). These high profile reformers, whether it is the Narasimham Committee which submitted its Report in 1998 or the Raghuram Rajan Report referred to above, share the following four characteristics. First, they are soaked in the market theology of the IMF/World Bank. Directed credit and credit subsidies should be shunned. Second, they demonstrate a congenital dislike of the public sector in the financial system. Third, their whole focus seems to be on mimicking the financial models of the West, particularly the American model. Fourth, they lack a sense of India's financial history. The author, for one, believes that Rajan Committee Report's recommended reforms are inconsistent with the strategy of inclusive growth embodied in the Eleventh Five-Year Plan (2007-2012).[1] The Committee's basic approach to financial sector reforms is flawed. The Report reflects faithfully the market theology of IMF/World Bank without taking into account the India-specific strength of public sector dominated financial system. For instance, 'The majority of this Committee does not see a compelling reason for continuing government ownership' of financial institutions including banks. In the global financial conflagration when icons of major private sector banks and financial institutions perished, Indian institutions stood rock-like unharmed. It is time that contemporary Indian policymakers 'unlearn' the market theology and refrain from mimicking the western financial models. Clearly, the Rajan Committee Report should be set aside. Perhaps it would be useful to set up a new Committee headed by a 'Dr. Reddy like expert' to provide an alternative blueprint for future financial sector reforms—reforms which would be in consonance of the inclusive growth strategy in the real sector.

American Bailout

It was earlier believed that the crisis of subprime mortgages in the US would be limited because this category of lending represented only 12 percentage of all home mortgages. But these loans triggered a full-blown financial crisis; because these were embedded in complex securities whose

1. Mujumdar (2008).

values and ownership were difficult to determine. The securitisation of debt process is described as a 'package of dodgy debts of some Alabama Unemployed Men turned into a High Grade Structured Enhanced Leverage Fund of a leading Wall Street Firm'.[2] Similar doubts afflicted other bonds. Demand for all such securities shrank and there was credit crunch. Lehman Brothers collapsed. The financial system had over-borrowed and underestimated the risks involved (see: Robert J. Samuelson, *Economic Times*, January 1, 2008).

There were other esoteric credit constructs and no wonder Warren Buffet called them weapons of mass destruction. The Ponzi scheme reached new heights in 2008, with the discovery of an alleged fraud that Barnard Madoff committed by duping some of the world's leading investment banks to the tune of $50 billion. May God save us from the predatory, free market forces!

The Keynesian intervention in a modified form was the solution to the collapse of the US system. Both the Federal government and the Federal Reserve had to come out with a massive bailout package. The Federal government rescued Citigroup and the Insurance giant AIG. The Federal Reserve pumped in more than $1 trillion in fresh credit. The Congress allotted $700 billion to the Treasury for the same purpose. Even the automobile giants including General Motors are among the beneficiaries of the rescue package.

Indian Initiatives

How did India respond to the emerging global scenario? To repeat, India is not facing a recession but an external sector-led slowdown. Two stimulus packages were announced. The first package announced on December 7, 2008, including a cut in excise duty by 4 per cent and raising of public expenditure by Rs. 20,000 crore to boost infrastructure development. The second package announced on January 2, 2009 was wide-ranging in its scope: enhancing spending power of states, offer of sops to exporters and small-scale sector, and raising the level of protection for cement and steel sectors.

2. Quoted by Tapan Babu in *Economic and Political Weekly*, November 8, 2008.

This fiscal package was reinforced by a series of monetary measures by Reserve Bank of India (RBI) designed to inject massive doses of liquidity in the system and bring down lending rates. So far, RBI has pumped in more than Rs. 30,000 crore through cuts in both cash reserve ratio (CRR) and statutory liquidity ratio (SLR); and also reduced its policy rates. As a cumulative result, commercial banks have brought down their lending rates.

In addition to the low interest rate regime, two other factors have brightened the prospects of sustainability of higher rates of GDP growth. First, the inflation rate has been almost halved from its peak of 12 per cent in August 2008. The wholesale price index (WPI) continued to decline for the ninth consecutive week and reached 5.91 per cent on December 27, 2008. Second, crude oil prices have shown a sharp fall from $147 per barrel in January 2008 to around $40.

While highlighting the brighter side of the Indian economic scenario, there are some issues which continue to cause concern and which cannot be overlooked. These include growing unemployment in export and export-related sub-sectors, and poor performance in manufacturing and export growth. The capital market has yet to regain the lost ground: the BSE Sensex which had reached peaks of 20,000 is now hovering around 10,000. The fiscal deficit is estimated to reach 5 per cent of GDP in 2008-09 as against the target of 3 per cent outlined in the Fiscal Responsibility and Budget Management Act (FRBM). Thus, Indian growth story sketched here is conditioned by these limitations.

References

Raghuram Rajan Committee (2008). *Draft Report of the Committee on Financial Sector Reforms (CFSR)*, New Delhi: Planning Commission, Government of India. April.

Mujumdar, N.A. (2008). "Next Generation Financial Sector Reforms and Inclusive Growth", in S. Subrahmanya and B.S. Bhandary (eds.), *Essays in honour of Prof. S.L.N. Simha*. Bangalore: Southern Economist.

26 The New Government

Focus on Broad-based, Decentralised Growth

The current chorus of the elite lobby seems to be that freed from the Marxist shackles, the new UPA government should rush in to implement liberalisation reforms—reforms left unfinished from its agenda of the previous term of office. What does this articulate lobby mean by reforms? Disinvestment, privatisation of public sector banks (PSBs); a bigger role for foreign direct investment (FDI) in retail, insurance, aviation and banking; dilution of government equity in profitably state-run entities; making Mumbai an international financial centre where multinationals could freely enter; merger of associate banks of the State Bank of India (SBI) with the parent bank so that this big bank could compete internationally based on the principle 'too big to fail', and so on.

Little do these advocates, who are pursuing these reforms with a theological passion, realise that we are now at a defining moment in the history of global financial system. The current global financial crisis and its impact on the real economy is ferocious and it has changed dramatically the institutional and policymaking landscape. Market fundamentalism embodied in neo-liberalism based on the notion that markets are self-correcting, allocate resources efficiently, and serve the public well, has collapsed. The state has a critical role to play in the management of the economy, including the financial sector.

Financial Sector

We may not have our own Reaganomics or Thatcherism to bury but our high profile reformers, whether it is the Narasimham Committee of 1998 or the Raghuram Rajan Committee of 2008, are soaked in the market theology of the IMF/World Bank. Take for instance, Raghuram Rajan Committee. 'The majority of this Committee does not see a compelling reason for continuing government ownership' of financial institutions, including banks. The Committee has therefore, recommended selling of small public sector banks (PSBs) to the private sector. In the light of the global financial crisis, how incongruous such baseless assertions sound! When the private sector icons of American and European financial system—commercial banks, investment banks, mortgage houses and insurance giants—collapsed like a pack of cards, Indian financial institutions dominated by the public sector, stood rock-like, unharmed. It is to the credit of Indian PSBs that they have been able to successfully blend the objectives of social banking with the market philosophy of optimising profitability. PSBs have made us proud. Our reformers must realise that banking efficiency is ownership neutral. There is very little intellectual support for privatisation of banks. In fact, the new thinking is that banks should be treated as public utilities. This chapter seeks to argue that the new government should, shedding the inherited baggage of ideological predilections, address the more mundane India-specific issues both in the financial and real sectors. This warrants a re-ordering of priorities. Let me illustrate.

The central question in financial sector reforms is: how should the financial system, particularly commercial banks, respond to the challenge of facilitating inclusive, or broad-based and decentralised growth in the real sector? The building up of a pyramid of rural lending institutions, including banks with all their multi-channels of credit delivery—this should be the core theme of the new discourse on financial sector reforms. Banks' resources may be enabled to reach rural borrowers, either directly or indirectly through the use of multiple channels such as self-help groups (SHGs), microfinance institutions (MFIs), NGOs, farmers' clubs, *panchayats* etc., as business facilitators or correspondents.

Second, the unorganised sector holds the key to broad-based decentralised growth. This sector contributes about 30 per cent of industrial production and about 40 per cent of exports. Despite occupying this central position, these microenterprises receive only 2 per cent of bank credit. Moreover, this sector has been affected adversely by the recent global financial crisis. The micro, small and medium enterprises (MSMEs) particularly related to exports like textiles and garments, gems and jewellery have been facing problems like slackness in demand for their products and delayed payments of dues by large undertakings. To ensure that the special problems faced by this sector are addressed, there is merit in the proposal to set up a dedicated development finance institution (DFI) with a mandate to provide refinance to banks for on-lending to microenterprises. Such an umbrella institution should be able, in addition to facilitating adequate flow of credit, to provide consultative services for upgradation of technology and improving marketing efficiency, and so on.

Third, a problem which none of the high profile reforms has addressed is the inequitable interest rate structure. Mindless implementation of Basel norms and adoption without adaptation of concepts like 'risks' as understood in developed world, has resulted in the emergence of an inequitable interest rate structure, designed to pamper the corporate elite and which is biased against the small borrowers generally. As the RBI Report (2006: 159) admits: 'to compensate for such Sub-BPLR lending other segments are charged higher rates of interest, thus leading to cross subsidization of the economically well-off borrowers by the economically poor borrowers'. This is indeed disturbing because it militates against inclusive growth and financial inclusion. Fortunately, RBI appointed in April 2009, a Working Group to review the whole BPLR system and submit the report in August 2009. One hopes that this distortion in interest rates would be corrected.

Real Sector

Turning to the real sector, I would briefly refer to three issues in the broad area of food and water security: watershed development, rural employment and food grains management policy. As Jeffrey Sachs has emphasised recently: 'Governments lose their legitimacy when they cannot guarantee their populations most basic needs: safe drinking water, staple food crops, and fodder and water for the animal herds on which communities depend for their meager livelihoods' (*Economic Times*, May 25, 2009).

First, even today about 60 per cent of the total cultivated area in India is rainfed and hence, future agricultural growth will have to be necessarily water-centric. I regard watershed development as the mother of all water management modes and today it is seen as the principal strategy for holistic development of rainfed areas. Even though we have made a lot of noise about this programme, in terms of dimensions involved, the progress is tardy. For instance, even in Maharashtra, which is a pioneer of this programme, only about 20 per cent of the potential area is covered by the programme. We should therefore promote a massive programme aimed at covering, say 50 per cent of the eligible area in the next two years. We could designate the two years 2009-10 and 2010-2011 as 'Watershed Development Years'.

Second, the National Rural Employment Guarantee Act (NREGA), 2005 is the best thing that could have happened to the rural poor. This guarantees 100 days of employment to every rural household. In 2008-09, it is estimated that about 4.5 crore rural households have benefited from the scheme. Rural connectivity, water harvesting structures, drought proofing, minor and micro-irrigation works are among the activities undertaken under the scheme. This scheme should be strengthened further and perhaps mandated to concentrate on watershed development activities in the next two years in the rainfed areas.

Taken together, these programmes would go a long way towards providing water and food security to the rural poor.

Third, in terms of food grains management policy we have not covered ourselves in glory. Ironically, India which is the abode of the largest number of chronically underfed and undernourished people in the world, exported a huge quantity of 27 million tonnes of food grains during the three consecutive years 2001-02 to 2003-04. This is another example of Indian policymakers of the period being soaked in market theology. What is worse, these policymakers made every effort to cut down the size of subsidies for domestic consumption of food grains but they had no qualms about subsidising exports of food grains! We seem to be refusing to learn from history. Wheat exports of some 2 million tonnes are again being permitted. One hopes that exports of wheat would not be subsidised! Recent FAO (2008) estimates show that the number of undernourished people in India has risen from 206.6 million in 1990-1992 to 230.5 million in 2003-2005, an increase of some 24 million. Domestic consumption needs must have the first claim on domestic production. Again, forward trading in wheat has been renewed and this does not portend well for wheat prices. In the Indian situation, farmers' decisions regarding investment in farming are guided by the minimum support prices (MSP), rather than by forward prices.

Hence, the agenda of the new government should reflect the concern for these rather mundane and India-specific issues.

References

RBI (2006). *Report on Currency and Finance, 2005-06*. RBI.

FAO (2008). *The State of Food Security in the World*. FAO.

27 Predatory Capitalism is Dead

Long Live Community-centred Capitalism!

The collapse of the American economy in 2008 was as traumatic as the collapse of Soviet Russia in 1991. Perhaps more traumatic because the US which is facing, as President-elect Barack Obama puts it: 'an economic crisis of historic proportions', is threatening to cause world recession in view of its dominance of the world economy. We have arrived at a moment in world economic history when the disillusionment with centrally planned economies is matched by disillusionment with the capitalist system led by unbridled market forces. We have discarded the centrally planned economic system and if we now disown the capitalist system, where do we go from here? To a no man's land?

Of course, it would be naive to believe that the alternative is between centrally planned economic system and the one led by unbridled market forces, because there are various versions of the two models. A more nuanced approach to the interpretation of the current mess in which many advanced countries find themselves today is warranted. Over the years, the capitalist system has deteriorated into a predatory capitalist system, as we would seek to demonstrate. The death-knell seems to have rung today for this predatory capitalist system. At the same time, we should recognise that some core elements of the capitalist system are needed to ensure sustained growth with equity. Hence, the search for a brand of sanitised capitalist system which would be sustainable. Thus the slogan: 'Predatory capitalism is dead: Long live community-centred capitalism!'

It is necessary to provide a clear interpretation of this situation because in the post-1990 reforms phase, Indian policymakers have demonstrated their total faith in the market theology of the IMF and the World Bank—a faith founded on unbridled market forces. It is this philosophy which is in shambles today.

The word 'predatory' is defined in simple terms as 'addicted to, or characterised by a tendency to exploit or destroy others for one's own gain'. The issue of predatory capitalism has assumed a contemporary relevance with the recent fall from grace of the American capitalistic image. Revelations of corporate crookedness and accounting scandals have shaken the very foundations of the American capitalist model. The depth of degradation to which unbridled corporate greed can lead has become all too obvious. The Enron, Worldcom and Xerox, and Global Crossing exposures have unveiled the ugly side of western style capitalism under which, in the quest for short-term gain, wrong doings are overlooked. These developments cannot be dismissed, as some apologists of American capitalism seem to be doing, as isolated incidents. As Prof. Lester C. Thurow puts it: 'The Enron, and Worldcom are not abnormalities in a basically sound system—scandals are endemic to capitalism'. The London Economist summed up the situation: 'Chief executives and accountants have become a despised breed less trusted than politicians and journalists' (The Economist, November 30, 2002). Take the current financial crisis in the US, which started as a subprime mortgage crisis. The litany of the actors involved and the sharp practices followed is long. The CEO of one of the bigger banks which was sinking helped himself to a hefty bonus. The automobile giants, Ford, Chrysler and General Motors went, in their private jets, to seed aid from the Congress. A fast growing new breed of lenders were luring many people into risky mortgages they could not afford. With incentives for aggressive loan disbursements, banks poured billions of dollars of loans into poor households often with incomplete documents. The unquestioned faith in the status of triple-A credit rating led to buying of billions of structured bonds which later turned out to be worth nothing, since the market for a number of structured products became non-existent during the period of financial meltdown. Thus it was not only mortgage houses, but also investment banks, accountants, and credit raters who were involved in the drama. For an excellent account of this financial chaos see article by Tapan Babu.[1] Have the financial professionals also joined the breed of CEOs mentioned above by *The Economist*?

Turning to the Indian scenario, two cases might be cited to illustrate the mistakes committed by our policymakers in their mindless pursuit of

1. *Economic and Political Weekly*, November 8, 2008.

market theology. India is the abode of the largest number of chronically underfed and undernourished persons in the world. And yet, we exported a huge quantity of 27 million tonnes of food grains during the three consecutive years 2001-02 to 2003-04. What is worse, following market theology, Indian policymakers cut down food subsidies for domestic consumers during this period. The same policymakers had no qualms about subsidising our exports of food grains! Could this be a textbook example of predatory capitalism?

It is an irony of history that such pervert policies were pursued in the land of Mahatma Gandhi. Nearly 100 years ago, the Mahatma emphasised: 'Basic human needs have the first claim on society's resources and it has an obligation to arrange its economic resources in a manner that the needs of all its members are met.'

The second example relates to the inequitable interest rate structure. Financial sector and banking sector reforms implemented in the 1990s have resulted in the emergence of an inequitable interest rate structure—a structure designed to pamper the corporate elite and which is biased against agricultural and the small borrower generally. For instance, a small farmer was made to pay an interest rate of 12 per cent at a time when a highly rated corporate entity could raise money from banks at 6 per cent. RBI's *'Report on Currency and Finance, 2005-06'* admits this point: 'To compensate for such sub-BPLR lending, other segments are charged higher rates of interest thus leading to cross subsidisation of economically well-off borrowers by the economically poor borrowers' (page 159).

Fortunately, all this is changing and social responsibility of the private corporate sector as well as the end-objectives of development are being redefined. Years ago, Milton Friedman wrote: 'There is one and only social responsibility of business—to use its resources and engage in activities designed to increase its profits.' Today, prophets of private sector philosophy disagree with Friedman. For instance, the Coca-Cola Chief who represents the not so pretty face of modern capitalism, scarred as it is by the recent Enron and Enron-like episodes, redefines corporate responsibility. As guest editor of the *Economic Times*, E. Neville Isdell wrote:

> The future of a 21st century company is tied to the health of our communities and our planet. Some leaders may consider sustainability work to be in a company's enlightened self-interest. I disagree. In ways that will determine our ability to achieve consistent, global growth and profitability it is quite literal self-interest
>
> (Editorial, March 17, 2008).

Water is the main ingredient in Coca-Cola and lack of public access to clean water is a serious problem in many communities where Coca-Cola factories are functioning. Hence, the objective of the Coca-Cola company has been to return water used in its manufacturing processes safely to the environment. In India, the company is installing more than 100 rain harvesting structures in 17 states. Thus community-centredness has become the focus of functioning of private corporate sector. The current crisis in the American and some other advanced economies should go a long way to further strengthen this philosophy.

The terms of public policy, building a strategy of inclusive growth in the real sector in the Eleventh Five-Year Plan (2007-2012) itself may be regarded as a correction of a policy guided primarily by unbridled market forces. The idea is to bring into the fold of development those sections of the population which the growth process has bypassed. Similarly, the RBI is vigorously pursuing a policy of financial inclusion bringing those communities which have remained excluded from the modern banking sector, into the financial mainstream. More recently, there was a massive farm loan write-off, of some Rs. 70,000 crore. Expanding the scope of the National Rural Employment Guarantee Act (NREGA) is another example of the concern for rural community. In the absence of a comprehensive social security scheme, the employment guarantee would provide some solace to the rural poor. Development policy is thus increasingly becoming community-centric.

Therefore, community-centred capitalism alone can ensure sustained growth with equity.

28 Dilemmas of the Central Bank

Introduction

The First Quarter Review of Monetary Policy 2009-10 was announced by Dr. D. Subbarao, Governor, Reserve Bank of India (RBI), on July 28, 2009. Unlike other quarterly reviews announced routinely, this review has an element of uniqueness about it, because it has to be appreciated in a broad global context.

We are living in extraordinary times. The global crisis which began as a crisis of the financial system in the US in 2008 subsequently engulfed most countries of the world. It had all the ingredients of a severe disruption of the world economy on the scale of the Great Depression of the 1930s. The International Monetary Fund (IMF) has projected that global trade will shrink by 12 per cent in 2009. The global growth forecast for 2009 is minus 1.3 per cent. However, the catastrophic consequences of a potential depression were mitigated by bold bailout packages offered in concert by both the governments and central banks in each country. For instance, Federal Reserve Chairman Ben S. Bernanke spelling out the rationale of such support said recently: 'In a financial crisis if you let the big firms collapse in a disorderly way, it will bring down the whole system... I was not going to be the Federal Reserve Chairman who presided over the second Great Depression'.

The Indian Economy

Fortunately, the Indian economy emerged largely unscathed from this global crisis. The worst hit was the export sector, which has been recording negative growth since October 2008. This in turn impacted the manufacturing sector. Services, which account for 64.5 per cent of GDP also experienced a modest slowdown. The financial sector, dominated by public sector institutions remained largely unaffected. GDP growth for

2008-09 was 6.7 per cent, reflecting deceleration from the average annual growth of 8.8 per cent recorded during the high growth phase of 2003-04 to 2007-08.

Policy Response

'Quick and aggressive policy responses both by the Government and Reserve Bank mitigated the adverse impact of the global financial crisis', asserts Dr. Subbarao. The large domestic demand bolstered by government's consumption, provision of forex and rupee liquidity coupled with sharp cuts in policy rates by Reserve Bank helped to soften the worst impact of the global crisis on the Indian economy. The government responded by providing three focussed fiscal stimulus packages in the form of tax relief to boost demand and increased expenditure on public projects to create employment and public assets. This fiscal stimulus amounted to Rs. 1,86,000 crore or 3.5 per cent of GDP at current market prices for 2008-09.[1] This fiscal accommodation led to an increase in fiscal deficit from 2.7 per cent in 2007-08 to 6.2 per cent in 2008-09.

On its part, RBI took a number of measures both to ease policy rates and enhance liquidity. For instance, the repo rate was reduced from 9 per cent to 4.75 per cent, reverse repo rate from 6 per cent to 3.25 per cent and cash reserve ratio (CRR) from 9 per cent to 5 per cent during the period October 2008 to July 2009. The release of primary liquidity since mid-September 2008 works out to a staggering figure of Rs. 5,61,700 crore.[2]

With these fiscal and monetary stimuli, it has been possible to sustain the GDP growth at 6 per cent with an upward bias in 2009-10. In a recession-riddled world, this is indeed an admirable achievement.

Dilemmas of Central Bank

The RBI faced the following four dilemmas:

First, the fiscal deficit rings an alarm bell. The fiscal deficit is projected to rise to 6.8 per cent in 2009-10, because of the factors

1. Budget Speech of Minister of Finance, Pranab Mukherjee, page 4.
2. See Table 20 in the Governor's Policy Statement.

mentioned above. The mandated targets under the Fiscal Responsibility and Budget Management (FRBM) Act, 2003 have thus been suspended. Again, the combined fiscal deficit of states for 2009-10 has risen to 3 per cent of GDP. Thus, taking the deficits of the Centre and states together, we end up with a figure of more than 9 per cent. For macroeconomic purposes, it is necessary to add to this the so-called below the line deficit—that is issue of bonds to oil marketing and fertiliser companies. The overall deficit thus works out to 11 per cent. Will this lead to higher inflation?

Second, the overhang of liquidity discussed above could fuel inflation. There is also a sizeable quantum of unutilised accommodation provided by RBI to banks; if this is fully utilised, there will be a surfeit of liquidity.

Third, the private corporate sector is vociferously lobbying for a further reduction in lending rates. This is despite the fact that the average effective lending rate has declined from 12.3 per cent in March 2008 to 11.1 per cent by March 2009. The Finance Minister has exhorted banks to reduce lending rates further. Dr. Subbarao also concedes the point: 'The banks have responded to the monetary stance by reducing deposit and lending rates, although there is scope for further reduction' (page 24). The critical issue here is: if deposit rates are further reduced, will it erode savings rate? In India, the household sector is a major contributor to overall financial savings and hence, one has to move cautiously in this area.

Fourth, the large government market borrowing programme of around Rs. 4,00,000 crore indicated in the Union Budget for 2009-10 has raised some apprehensions about government crowding out the private sector. Dr. Subbarao has explained that nearly 63 per cent of the borrowing programme for the first half of the year has already been completed and hence, there is enough elbow room for the RBI to manage the balance borrowing smoothly.

Maintaining the Status Quo

Keeping these dilemmas in mind, Dr. Subbarao chose wisely to maintain the status quo. That is, the policy rates remained unchanged: the bank rate at 6 per cent; repo rate at 4.75 per cent; reverse repo rate at 3.25 per cent; and cash reserve ratio at 5 per cent. The stance of monetary policy will be to maintain a monetary and interest rate regime consistent with price stability and financial stability supportive of returning the economy to the high growth path.

The Inflation Puzzle

Inflation measured by wholesale price index (WPI) was minus 1.17 per cent on July 11, 2009. But this is a statistical illusion. As Subbarao explains, 'The currently observed negative WPI inflation largely reflects the statistical effect of the high base of last year and should not be interpreted as structural deflation arising from demand contraction'. In fact for the first time, RBI has given a breakdown of the inflation data which indicates that essential commodities have recorded a price rise of 10.6 per cent on July 11, 2009 as compared to the level a year ago. This is further corroborated by the fact that inflation as measured by the consumer price index (CPI) shows a rise of about 11 per cent. The divergence between WPI and CPI inflation rates has become more pronounced in the recent period and hence, the credibility of WPI as a policy tool has been eroded. This also underlines the need to evolve an index which would faithfully reflect the movements in prices of essential commodities included in the consumer basket of an average household.

Overall, the current global crisis has generated extraordinary circumstances and these in turn warrant extraordinary policy responses.

Part V

The Agricultural Sector

29 Commodity Futures Market

Dehyphenating Financial Flows and Supply-Demand Fundamentals

Futures trading in agricultural commodities does not seem to have attracted much academic interest in India. Of course, the macroeconomic functions and utility of commodities futures trading are well established. But, many times we seem to be swept away by the textbook market theology, with an inadequate understanding of the underlying processes of futures trading and its broader implications for macroeconomic management of the agricultural economy, particularly in the India-specific situation. Futures trading in agricultural commodities, particularly food grains, has certain unique features as contra-distinguished from say, trading in metals like copper or gold. It has broader implications for food prices and food security, rural employment and reduction of poverty. The decision-making process in the farm sector, unlike in a corporate entity, is dispersed widely over a large number of small farmers, spread throughout the length and breadth of the country-farmers who are perhaps yet to be sensitised to futures prices. What is the transmission mechanism by which market signals are sought to be transmitted to the average farmer? Does such a mechanism already exist and, if not, how do we propose to go about building such an apparatus? There is a more fundamental question regarding prices, both spot, and future. Prices do play a role in impacting production, but perhaps a limited role in an agricultural economy characterised by supply rigidities.

More concretely, let us discuss the issue with reference to the two main functions of the commodity derivative market, namely price discovery and risk management. For instance, it is argued: 'derivative markets neither raise prices nor depress them. They just discover prices in the light of the present and prospective supply and demand.'[1] What are the

1. *Commodities Vision*, MCX Academia of Economic Research, Editorial, p.8, July 2007.

ground realities? This question becomes particularly relevant the context of the phenomenal growth of turnover of the futures contracts witnessed since 2003. In fact Prof. Kabra (2007) estimates that the volume of futures trade in commodities has surpassed the total turnover of 150-year old stock exchanges. Although it is difficult to have precise estimates, the quantum of financial resources involved in futures trading is said to be astronomical. All this has happened in the absence of any quantum jump in the production of agricultural commodities. In effect this would be tantamount to what can be called dehyphenating of financial flows in the commodity's futures market and the supply and demand fundamentals of the commodities concerned. Can this recent phenomenon be interpreted to mean that the futures market has taken a new avatar, as it were, abdicating its primary function of equilibrating supply and demand of commodities over a period? What happens to the so-called 'price discovery', under these circumstances? Has the voyage of 'price discovery' metamorphosed into a voyage of 'price determination?' In simplistic terms, inflation has been defined as 'too much money chasing too few goods'. Is the present situation in the commodities futures market analogous to the definition? There is a strong view that stock markets have ceased to be barometers of the state of the economy concerned. Has the same fate befallen the commodities futures market in its new avatar? These are some of the disturbing questions which need to be addressed.

Second, regarding price risk management function, it is claimed that 'a commodity derivative market has a built-in mechanism for stabilising the physical market prices that are prone to fluctuate in response to unpredictable shifts in supply and demand'.[2] Textbook theology apart, the basic India-specific characteristic, which is often overlooked in such discussions is the existence of the system of minimum support prices (MSP) for several agricultural commodities. The average farmer is fully aware of the MSP and also has come to anticipate that the levels of MSPs would go on rising over the years. This itself takes away the sting of the so-called price risk management. In the absence of a transmission of mechanism, the question of the average farmer responding to futures prices in terms of pre-sowing and past-harvest decisions does not arise. Of course, there might be some isolated cases of 'success stories' of farmers benefiting

2. See Footnote 1, p.9.

from futures markets but we are really focussing on the large mass of farmers.

Historically, the track record of private trade in say, food grains does not cover itself in glory. When food grains trade was the exclusive domain of private trade what used to happen was: prices were depressed in immediate post-harvest period and they rose significantly in the lean period. The bulk of the small farmers with little holding power were compelled to sell the produce at these depressed un-remunerative prices. Consumers had to pay high prices for food grains in the lean season. Thus, both producers and consumers were the losers and the trader was the gainer. This phenomenon has become part of folklore of textbooks on the Indian economy. It was only with the emergence of the Food Corporation of India (FCI), as the countervailing power in food grains trade, that the amplitude of seasonal variations in food grains prices was substantially reduced. Taken together, these two policy interventions, namely MSP and FCI procuring food grains at support prices, have been admirably performing the function of price risk management for the farming community as a whole.

The euphoria about globalisation has led some experts to advocate integration of Indian commodity markets with global markets. As Goyal (2007) puts it: 'Hence, there is a need to integrate our agricultural production with national and international markets to enable farmers to benefit from higher prices'. The underlying idea appears to be that futures market could provide such a link. These experts seem to overlook the fact that international agricultural prices are a huge mess. They neither reflect the true costs of production nor supply and demand fundamentals, distorted as they are by massive subsidies given to agriculture in the US and European Union countries. Despite protracted negotiations at the WTO, we are unable to persuade these countries to reduce these subsidies, let alone eliminate them. Against this broader background, to judge Indian agriculture's international competitiveness with reference to distorted international prices has hardly any meaning.

One final word about structural supply rigidities to which I referred earlier. In eulogising the role of commodities futures, sometimes we seem to deify the role of price as a magic wand which would transform commodity deficits into commodity surpluses. This impression needs to be corrected. More recently, the world over, food prices have been rising substantially contributing to rise in consumer prices and thereby to inflation in general. For instance, global wheat prices in July 2007 were 52 per cent above the average prices prevailing during the calendar year 2004 and rice prices were 38 per cent higher. A new term 'agflation' has been coined to describe this phenomenon of food prices fuelling inflation. This cannot be explained in terms of the 'monetary phenomenon' or the phenomenon of temporary 'supply-demand' imbalances. Structural constraints like global warming, rigidities in water and land supplies, have become more prominent. Again, there are new elements on the scenario like fast growing biofuels industry which also reinforce the constraint. For instance, Peskett *et al.* (2007) view that, 'bio-fuels will result in increased hunger as maize is diverted away from household food utilisation in developing countries to feed the cars of households in the developed world starving the people to feed Cars?'.

That is why Rabinovitch (2007) points out: 'Forecasting the future of food prices is more the realm of the agronomist than the economist'. According to a recent joint assessment by the OECD and FAO, global prices of agricultural commodities are likely to rule higher than their historic equilibrium levels over the next 10 years.[3]

The simple lesson is that we cannot bring about a second Green Revolution in India by using the instrument of price alone.

We have to therefore address the issue of how structural supply rigidities circumscribe the role of prices, spot and futures, in influencing production.

References

Kabra, Kamal Nayan (2007). "Commodity Futures in India", *Economic and Political Weekly*: 1165. March 31.

Goyal, Prashant (2007). "Signals from Futures", *Economic Times*, September 6.

Peskett, L., R. Slater, C. Stevens and A. Dufey (2007). "Biofuels, Agriculture and Poverty Reduction", *Natural Resource Perspective* 107. UK: ODI, June.

Rabinovitch, S. (2007). "Agflation takes root in tracking world price swings", *Economic Times*, May 16.

---

3. Annual Report, Reserve Bank of India, 2006-07.

Opening Remarks at the Seminar "Futures Trading in Agricultural Commodities—Its Impact on Agricultural Production and Prices", Mumbai University, Mumbai, September 28, 2007.

30 Tryst with the Monsoon

Textbooks on Indian economy of my generation used to describe Indian agriculture as a 'gamble in monsoons'. The hype built up by the media on the delay in the arrival of monsoon this year makes us wonder whether after nearly six decades of development planning, we are any better off today than what we were prior to, say 1951. Because of the late start, the country as a whole received only 50 per cent of the normal rainfall upto June 23, 2009. This has led to shrill crises of 'drought' or 'famine' staring at us. No doubt there are some distress pockets like the north, the west which received only 21 per cent of the normal rainfall, or Vidarbha in Maharashtra. But it is necessary to take a holistic view of the outlook for the year 2009-10. Fears are expressed that GDP growth may decline to 5 per cent in 2009-10 from the level of 6 plus per cent during the previous two years. The spectre of food prices-led inflation is hovering around us, we are told. Inflation as measured by the consumer price index (CPI) has already touched 10.2 per cent in May 2009. Fiscal deficits of a sizeable magnitude have already been factored into the budgets of 2008-09 and 2009-10. Is this lethal combination of large fiscal deficits and supply shortages of food grains not a recipe for hyper inflation? Would we be compelled to import food grains on a large scale? Will the green shoots, which some economists see as reflecting the return of the Indian economy to a high growth trajectory of 8 or 9 per cent, be blighted by the impending agricultural slump?

Fortunately, these fears were quelled by the Indian Meteorological Department (IMD), which announced its long-range forecast update for the 2009 southwest monsoon, on June 24, 2009: 'Quantitatively, monsoon rainfall for the country as a whole is likely to be 93 per cent of the long-term period average, with model error of 4 per cent + or –. Further, IMD asserted: 'Yes, there is a 50 per cent rainfall deficiency but that is not a drought—like situation under any circumstances. Sufficient rainfall in July which is the key month for sowing, may cover the June deficit'. IMD also downplayed the role of E1 Nino in the poor progress of monsoon.

Extenuating Circumstances

Although the forecast of 'below normal' monsoon is worrying, there is no cause for panic. There are several extenuating factors to support this point. First, we begin the year 2009-10 with a comfortable food grains supply situation. We have had two successive years 2007-08 and 2008-09 of good harvest, with food grains output of 230 million tonnes in both the years. As a result, it was possible to procure a high quantity of rice of nearly 31 million tonnes and nearly 25 million tonnes of wheat. At present, food grains stocks with the government exceed 50 million tonnes; this quantity is twice the storage capacity of the Food Corporation of India (FCI). Second, as a consequence of this large procurement, government seems to have committed to export 2 million tonnes of wheat. It was also contemplating export of 2 million tonnes of rice, before the alarm bell regarding the current year's monsoon began ringing. One thing is now clear: no exports of food grains should be permitted, except marginal exports of high-value *basmati* rice. Thus, we will have a high enough cushion to meet any eventuality of shortfall in food grains production in 2009-10. Third, south-west monsoon affects *kharif* crops which account for about 50 per cent of total food grains. Upto June 2009, out of 36 meterological subdivisions, rainfall was excess-to-normal in 8 divisions but deficient-to-scanty in 28 divisions. This does not justify the alarmistic view that because of delayed monsoon 'all is lost'. Thus, this year is more akin to 2004-05 than the year 2002-03. Drought was widespread in 2002-03 when food grains production declined sharply by 18 per cent, from 218 million tonnes during the previous year to 175 million tonnes. On the other hand, in 2004-05, when drought was limited to some states, food grains production declined by only 7 per cent. Fourth, in terms of impact of agricultural slump on GDP, the overall situation is far from alarming. For the last five years, the annual average growth of GDP was 8.5 per cent, with agriculture recording 3.5 per cent growth. Even taking the pessimistic scenario of agricultural growth dipping to 2 per cent in 2009-10, its impact on GDP would be around 0.3 per cent, since agriculture contributes only 18 per cent to overall GDP. Thus, GDP growth in 2009-10 may turn out to be some 5.8 per cent. Fifth, the decline in agricultural growth may be compensated by the export sector which also accounts for some 15 per cent of GDP. The Federal Reserve has confirmed that the US recession is ceasing. The OECD in its latest *Economic Outlook* has indicated that the economic slump in the European Union is bottoming out. These developments should encourage India's exports which had dipped to their lowest levels last year. This must be factored into any forecast of GDP for 2009-10. Again, there are definite indicators that the growth rates in manufacturing and construction are accelerating. Cumulatively, these trends may boost GDP growth to some 7 per cent. In fact, the World Bank's forecast for India's GDP growth in 2010 was 8 per cent.

Finally, international fertiliser prices have declined sharply from their peak levels reached last year. This should promote application of optimum doses of fertilisers to crops, thereby boosting crop yields this year.

Food Grain Prices and Inflation

The usual textbook formula of output-money-prices cannot be blindly applied to the food grain prices in India, basically because food grains market in India is a segmented market. The public distribution system (PDS) caters to sizeable population where food grain prices are subsidised. Similarly, the mid-day meal programme covers some 15 crore children. The National Food Security Act proposed by the President of India in her Address to Parliament on June 4, 2009, seeks to provide a statutory basis for a framework which assures food security for all. Every family below the poverty line (BPL) in rural as well as urban areas will be entitled, by law, to 25 kg of rice or wheat per month at Rs. 3/kg. Preliminary work in this legislation is under way and the forthcoming budget is expected to provide Rs. 50,000 crore for the programme.

These social safety nets insulate the vulnerable sections of the population from prices in the open market for food grains.

Policy Implications

The media is full of agonising tales of water and power shortages in some pockets of the country. This demonstrates clearly that we do not have any contingency plans, both at the macro and micro levels, to meet problems caused by the delay in the monsoon. We do not seem to learn from history!

Be that as it may, I would seek to highlight, in terms of medium-term policy implications, three issues: (i) export of food grains, (ii) food grains management, and (iii) watershed development.

First, there should be no exports of food grains, except some small quantities of high value commodities like *basmati* rice. Soaked in market theology, our policymakers exported a huge quantity of 27 million tonnes of food grains during the three consecutive years 2001-02 to 2003-04. India is the abode of the largest number of chronically underfed and undernourished people in the world. Against this background, massive exports of food grains remain historically as a monument of mindless pursuit of market theology. Wisdom seems to have dawned on us at last, as reflected in the proposed Food Security Act, referred to above.

Second, the Food Corporation of India (FCI) needs to play a more proactive role in the management of food grains prices. We seem to treat the FCI as a glorified godown keeper. Instead, it should emerge as a market maker. For instance, with its huge stocks of rice and wheat, it should ensure that food grains prices in the open market do not rise to high levels. It should be able to identify pockets of high price rises and by unloading appropriate quantities of food grains in those pockets, it should seek to bring down prices. In other words, it should be possible to contain food grains prices within a reasonable band, irrespective of fiscal deficits.

Finally, it is not unavailability of food grains, or of foreign exchange but unavailability of water which is going to act as a constraint on India's future economic growth. Even today, about 60 per cent of the total cultivated area is rainfed and hence future agricultural growth will be necessarily water-centric. In terms of immediacy, watershed development can be regarded as the mother of all water management modes. Medium and large irrigation projects have a large gestation period, and involve large investments. Water harvesting and conservation have become imperative. Watershed development has therefore emerged as the principal strategy for holistic development of rainfed areas. Even though we have been making a lot of noise about this programme, progress is tardy. If anxieties of this year's monsoon have taught us any lesson it is this: promote a massive programme of watershed development, both macro and micro, aimed at covering say, 50 per cent of the potential area in the next two years. In fact, workers under the National Rural Employment Guarantee Act (NREGA), could be mandated to address this task in the rainfed areas. Only such a programme addressed on war footing could provide water and food security to the bulk of the poor.

Index

D

E

F

S

T

U

W